JOB INTERVIEW

How to Turn Job Interviews Into Job Offers

MARTIN YATE, CPC
New York Times bestselling author

A adamsmedia

AVON, MASSACHUSETTS

Dedication

When you turn job interviews into job offers, new and wonderful things become possible in your life. In the year it took to write, edit, and publish this book, I got engaged to and married Angela, who has given me the opportunity to make new and wonderful things happen in my life. Angela, this book is for you.

Acknowledgments

The *Knock 'em Dead* books are a team project in every sense of the word. My considerable thanks to Will Yate for his attention to detail and editorial insight; to Karen Cooper, Peter Archer, and the team at Adams Media; and to all the fans of the *Knock 'em Dead* books, who make the whole thing shine for me every day.

Published by
Adams Media, a division of F+W Media, Inc.
57 Littlefield Street, Avon, MA 02322.
U.S.A.
www.adamsmedia.com

ISBN 10: 1-4405-3679-1
ISBN 13: 978-1-4405-3679-3

Printed in the United States of America.

10 9 8 7 6 5 4 3 2 1

Library of Congress Cataloging-in-Publication Data
Yate, Martin John.
  Knock 'em dead job interview / Martin Yate.
  p. cm.
  ISBN 978-1-4405-3679-3 (pbk.) – ISBN 1-4405-3679-1 (pbk.)
1. Employment interviewing. 2. Job hunting. I. Title. II. Title: Knock them dead job interview.
  HF5549.5.I6Y373 2012
  650.14'4–dc23
                 2012027868

CONTENTS

THE LAW OF SURVIVAL

IF YOU LIVED IN THE WILD, you'd need to know how to make fire to survive. But you live in an urban world, and you need to make money. That means you need a job, and the only way you get a job is by turning a job interview into a job offer.

The transition you are going through today probably isn't your first job change, and it probably won't be your last, either. Statistics say that you will likely change jobs about every four years throughout your work life, and since you'll probably work for about fifty years, that means 12–15 job changes. With so many job changes throughout the average career, it should be a no-brainer that job search and career management skills are the most important skills you can possess. However, throughout your life you've been told that all you need to do is get an education, and the rest will take care of itself. The ability to turn a job interview into a job offer—the equivalent of the caveman's ability to make fire—is the most important skill you can ever possess, and yet no one has ever bothered to teach it to you. And because of that, what should be your greatest strength has become your greatest liability.

In this *Knock 'em Dead* book, I am going to show you how to turn this critical weakness into a strength: I'm going to show you *how to turn job interviews into job offers*. Going forward, you will use the strategies and tactics you learn here not just to get a job, but to improve your career: These are skills you will be thankful for throughout your life.

Why Do You Go to Job Interviews?

Headhunters and hiring managers say that many candidates think interviews are about deciding whether they want the job, and that often the only questions asked are about salary, vacation, and benefits. *You don't go to a job interview to decide if you want the job*, because you have nothing to decide until an offer is put on the table.

You go to a job interview to get a job offer and to turn your greatest professional weakness—turning job interviews into job offers—into a professional strength.

Nothing else matters, not the pay, the benefits, or the work environment; they are all irrelevant until an offer is on the table. You go to every job interview to improve your ability to get job offers, so you should treat every interview as an opportunity to build this most critical survival skill.

Interviewers Hate Interviewing

The person on the other side of the desk is not your adversary; she's someone who really wants to hire you. The truth is, managers hate interviewing. They want to find someone who *can* do the work, *wants* to do the work, and can get along with others. They want to hire someone ASAP and get back to their real work.

You just have to help them make that decision, and that is what I am going to help you do. Listen up, because I am not going to waste a word, or a moment of your time. Remember, what you learn will not only help you land that next job, it can change the trajectory of your life.

PART ONE

How to Turn Job Interviews Into Job Offers

CHAPTER 1

THE FIVE SECRETS BEHIND EVERY HIRING DECISION

As you walk in the door for your next interview, I guarantee that hiring manager is thinking, *"Please* let this be the one I can hire so I can get back to my real job." How well you perform in job interviews determines the jobs you are offered, the money you earn and, to a degree, the life you enjoy outside of work: You want to do this well. Your job search is a sales campaign, and job interviews are sales presentations. Whatever you do professionally, for the duration of your job search you have another job title: You are a salesperson selling *the professional you*—a unique portfolio of skills, experience, behaviors, and values wrapped in a living, breathing package that qualifies you to do a specific job particularly well. You are selling a living product: yourself.

At job interviews, you display your product for potential buyers. These buyers—your interviewers—compare your product to the others they have seen. How effectively you pitch your product and differentiate it from the others will determine whether or not you get the job offer.

The Building Blocks of Job Offers

The ability to turn interviews into offers is built from the following components:

- Understanding how your customers make buying decisions
- Understanding what your customers want to buy
- Identifying what you have for sale that they want to buy
- Tailoring your sales pitch to your customer's needs
- Selling what you have to offer

Preparation is half the work: Prepare properly and succeed; or don't, and fail. To differentiate yourself from other candidates, you've first got to understand how your customers make their buying decisions. This is especially important because the criteria employers use to make hires are the same ones they use to decide who gets the raises and promotions.

How Employers Make Buying Decisions

No employer wakes up in the morning saying, "It's a wonderful day in the neighborhood; I think I'll hire an accountant." Staff is only ever added to the payroll for one reason: *to help the company make money.* Whatever your job title, that job is a small but important cog in the complex moneymaking machinery of the corporation.

Your cog has its own set of responsibilities and contributions to make, but it must also mesh seamlessly with other cogs in the department (and elsewhere in the company), working in harmony to execute tasks beyond the scope of individual effort. Your job title is only added to the payroll when the costs of hiring and paying you are outweighed by your contribution to the bottom line, through bringing money into the company, saving money, saving time, or otherwise increasing productivity.

There are five criteria that hiring managers apply to every hiring decision to ensure these goals are met. These criteria are applied when hiring for any job, at any level and in every profession. Understanding these five secrets of the hire will change the way you think about your work, revolutionize your performance at job interviews, and can power greater success in your next job and throughout your career.

The First Secret: Ability and Suitability

Saying, "Hey, I can do this job—give me a shot and I'll prove it to you," is not enough to land a job offer. You have to prove it by demonstrating a combination of all the skills that define your ability to do that job. You bring two broad sets of skills to any job:

1. You must demonstrate an *ability* to do the work: that you are in full possession of the *technical skills* necessary to execute the job's responsibilities, and that you have a clear grasp of the role your job plays in the department, as that small but important cog in that complex moneymaking machinery of the corporation.

2. You must also establish your *suitability* for the job. You possess a body of profession/industry knowledge that helps you understand "the way things get done in banking/agribusiness/pharmaceuticals." This *profession/industry knowledge* differs from one industry to the next and it must be obvious that you speak the language, know the protocols, and understand the challenges that your industry exists to help people solve.

For example, a computer programmer working in a bank has *technical skills*. She shows *ability* to do the job by demonstrating possession of coding skills in different programming languages and how to apply them in writing good code for specific applications.

This programmer shows *suitability* for the job by demonstrating an understanding of how the program will be used in application and why it will be used that way. This understanding comes from a *familiarity with the operations of banking, the unique needs that banking operations generate,* and the terminology used to communicate in banking. Familiarity with these *industry-specific* considerations has considerable impact on that programmer's ability to do a satisfactory job.

The Reality of Industry Bias

But wait, you say, a computer programmer doesn't have to know banking: He can pick that up fairly quickly. It's the programming skills that are important. I don't disagree, but if you were the hiring manager, and you had to pick between two programmers with equal technical skills, identical except for the fact that one candidate comes from your industry and the other doesn't, which would you choose? It's a no-brainer: You'd choose the one who knows your business.

When employers interview candidates from other industries, they first look for the *technical skills* used to execute the responsibilities of the job. If you've gotten as far as the interview, *you clearly have many of these skills.* Your issue now becomes one of "suitability": your industry-specific understanding of *why things get done the way they do.*

The Causes of Industry Bias

Every industry develops distinctive characteristics in response to the unique qualities of the service it delivers to customers. Every company is engaged in industry-specific methodologies and challenges, and there are always idiosyncratic situations and sensitivities that arise from the nature of that industry's product or service. Industries naturally develop their own languages, priorities, and *ways of doing things* in response to their needs.

Industry bias springs from real concerns about a candidate's understanding of the building blocks of commerce in the new industry: the industry jargon, the myriad problems likely to crop up on the job every day, and the working relationships necessary to execute on the company's promise of excellent service or product.

A candidate who doesn't *understand the language* of the new industry almost certainly won't be sensitive to the other industry-specific challenges and the methodologies developed in response. This candidate is seen as having a longer, steeper learning curve, which means more time and money in training and greater odds of a failed hire, both of which managers prefer to avoid because these costs lead to failed managers.

What can you do to overcome this industry bias if switching industries is part of your job search plan and you are stalling out in job interviews?

The Solutions to Industry Bias

You already have many of the *technical, critical thinking,* and *problem-solving skills* of the new job; what you lack is that intuitive *feel* for how your work fits into the overall moneymaking machinery of this particular industry. Understanding the unique challenges posed by the services the new industry exists to satisfy—the needs of the clients, vendors, colleagues, and coworkers with whom you and your work interact—will be at the core of both your research into the new industry and your subsequent positioning at job interviews.

How do you deal with this? Give yourself a "new industry 101" orientation course. Take the time to understand the unique qualities of service that define your target industry and the challenges these present to the workers within the industry.

Identify people already doing this work: They can educate you about these issues, and tell you why things work the way they do. You can ask these questions of contacts in your alumni or professional association, your professional networks, or on industry/profession-specific groups on LinkedIn. You can also search databases on LinkedIn and other social networking sites for people who have made similar transitions.

The insights you gather will enable you to understand your future place in your new industry. (How you use social networks to help you do this is beyond the scope of this book, but it is detailed in the latest edition of *Knock 'em Dead: The Ultimate Job Search Guide.*)

When an employer sees your grasp of industry-specific issues and protocols, the risks associated with hiring you will diminish.

The Second Secret: Every Job Is about Problem Anticipation, Identification, Prevention, and Solution

As we have seen, there is only one reason any job is ever added to the payroll of a company, and that is to help the company make money. Jobs do this by bringing money into the company, saving money, improving productivity in some way, or through some combination of these activities.

This mandate of contributing to the profitability of the company in some small way is at the heart of every job. Take a few moments to determine whether your job is chiefly concerned with generating revenue, protecting assets, improving productivity in some way, or is perhaps a combination of these imperatives.

The day-to-day realities of your working week—the real meat of your work—involve:

- Identifying and preventing problems that limit your contributions to the bottom line.
- Creating timely and efficient solutions to the problems that cannot be avoided.

So, regardless of profession or title, at some level we are all hired to do the same job: We are all problem solvers, paid to *anticipate, prevent, and solve problems* within our areas of expertise. This applies to any job, at any level, in any organization, and in every profession.

Your challenge at a job interview is to show how *your efforts support these goals*. You can start work on this by creating a comprehensive list of the typical problems you tackle on a daily basis. Then for each item on your list, identify:

1. The ways you execute your responsibilities every day to prevent this problem from arising in the first place.
2. Early warning signals you look for and the actions you take to nip these problems in the bud, before they get any worse.

3. How you tackle the full-blown problems that arr
   desk every day anyway.

Repeat this exercise for every item on your list, then look at your work and see if you can identify certain methodologies common to all of them.

The next step is to review what you have learned about the challenges of your job and how you handle them, and tweak them just a little further so that you can use them in conversation at job interviews. Here's an approach you can use to develop examples of your problem-solving skills in action, and the resulting solutions and their benefits:

1. State the problem. What was the situation? Was it typical of your job, or had something unusual occurred?
2. What was the cause of the problem? Isolate relevant background information.
3. What was the desired outcome?
4. What skills did you bring into play to tackle this problem?
5. Recall the solution. How did things turn out in the end? Who benefited and how?
6. If you can, quantify the solution in terms of money earned, money saved, or time saved or productivity increased. Specify your role as either a team member or a lone gun.

The second secret of the hire tells you that whatever your job title, you are hired to *anticipate, prevent, and solve problems* within your areas of expertise. Your task at a job interview is to show how *your efforts support these goals.* That's exactly what these exercises help you do.

The Third Secret: The Transferable Skills That Underlie Professional Success

Successful professionals are simply people who crack the code of professional success and apply what they learn. There is, in fact, a set of *transferable skills* and *professional values common to all jobs,* which help you do your job well. They are the foundation of all professional success, informing your actions, judgment, ethics, and interaction with others.

The Transferable Skills	The Professional Values
Technical	*Motivation and Energy*
Critical Thinking	*Commitment and Reliability*
Communication	*Determination*
Multitasking	*Pride and Integrity*
Creativity	*Productivity*
Teamwork	*Systems and Procedures*
Leadership	

You see these words and phrases in job postings all the time; they are so common that they often seem to have lost all meaning. In fact, they are the skills and values that help you do whatever it is you do, well.

It is your embodiment of these *transferable skills* and *professional values* in everything you do that conveys professional competence; they are the skills that build reputations and success. They get you hired, get you noticed, land you top assignments, and lead to promotions and raises; they enable you to succeed in all your professional endeavors because they are the building blocks of success.

When you show your possession of *transferable skills* and *professional values* at job interviews, you give your answers substance, the ring of truth, and a tone that chimes p-r-o-f-e-s-s-i-o-n-a-l. We will talk about them in greater detail in the next chapter.

The Fourth Secret: Intelligent Enthusiasm

In a tightly run job race, when there is nothing to choose between two top candidates, the job offer will always go to the most *intelligently enthusiastic* candidate. The problem is that interviews are stressful situations, and when you are stressed, your defenses are up and you retreat behind a wall of stiff professionalism; the natural enthusiasm and motivations normally part of your professional persona are restrained.

However, employers see *intelligent enthusiasm* for your work as a signal that you are someone who is motivated to do a good job. This is expressed by more than smiles and saying you want the job; it is expressed by your deep understanding and respect for your work and its challenges, as well as your obvious relish in tackling those challenges every day.

It is also expressed by your genuine engagement in the work through the questions you ask. Interviewers make judgments of professional competency based partly on candidates' statements about the work they do, and partly on the questions those candidates ask, because those questions display a depth of understanding that statements cannot.

From the employer's side of the desk, the preference for motivated, *intelligently enthusiastic* candidates is roughly this:

- The *intelligently enthusiastic* candidate will work harder and will turn in a superior work product.
- Someone who really enjoys his work and is engaged in his profession will be easier to work with, and that will be a positive influence and a welcome, happy addition to the team.
- Your display of a *deep understanding and respect for your work and its challenges, and your obvious relish in tackling those challenges every day*, reinforces your understanding of the problems that lie at the heart of the job and your ability to handle them.
- This *intelligent enthusiasm* speaks to a professional commitment that is more likely to be backed up by technical competency and

the possession of the *transferable skills* and *professional values* that make for good hires.

• Someone who is intelligently enthusiastic and motivated by her work is likely to have a greater understanding of the job and therefore a greater commitment to taking the rough with the smooth.

Let this fourth secret of the hire encourage you to allow your natural enthusiasm for your work and for this job opportunity to shine through, rather than hide it because of interview nerves or a misconstrued sense of professionalism.

When it comes to a tightly run job race between equally qualified candidates, *the offer will always go to the most intelligently enthusiastic candidate.* Show enthusiasm for your work, your profession, and the opportunity; it just might be the tiebreaker that delivers your ideal job.

The Fifth Secret: Teamwork and Manageability

Teamwork relates to your ability to function productively as a member of a group focused on achieving large-scale goals. Working on a team takes patience, balance, tolerance, and an ability to assert your own personality without overpowering everyone else's. You don't have to *like* everyone on your team; but you have to make the effort to *work* with them productively. Your willingness to be a team player and your ability to function as an integrated member of the team is critical because many of the contributions your department must make toward the smooth running of the corporate machine are beyond the scope of your individual contribution.

CHAPTER 2

THE FOUNDATIONS OF
CAREER SUCCESS

UNDERSTAND WHAT YOUR CUSTOMERS WANT TO BUY. There are certain key words relating to skills that you see in almost every job posting: communication, multitasking, teamwork, creativity, critical thinking, leadership, determination, productivity, motivation, and a few more we'll discuss shortly. These words represent a secret language that few job hunters ever show that they understand. The ones who do "get it" are also the ones who get the job offers.

That is because, as discussed in the previous chapter, these key words and phrases represent the skills that enable you to do your job well, whatever your job may be. They are known as *transferable skills* and *professional values* because no matter what the job, the profession, or the elevation of that job, these skills and values make the difference between success and failure.

The Professional Everyone Wants to Work With

Over the years, I've read a lot of books about finding jobs, winning promotions, and managing your career. One theme that runs through many of them is just plain harmful: the advice to "just be yourself." Wrong. Remember that first day on your first job, when you went to get your first cup of coffee? You found the coffee machine, and there, stuck on the wall behind it, was a handwritten sign reading:

YOUR MOTHER DOESN'T WORK HERE
PICK UP AFTER YOURSELF

You thought, "Pick up after myself? Gee, guess I've got to develop a new way of doing things." And so you started to observe and emulate the more successful professionals around you. You weren't born this way. You developed new skills and ways of conducting yourself, in effect creating a *professional persona* that enabled you to survive in the professional world.

There is a specific set of *transferable skills* and *professional values* that underlies professional success: skills and values that employers all over the world in every industry and profession are anxious to find in candidates from the entry-level to the boardroom. Why this isn't taught in schools and in the university programs that cost a small fortune is unfathomable, because these skills and values are the foundation of every successful career. They break down into these groups:

1. *The Technical Skills of Your Current Profession*

These are the technical competencies that give you the *ability* to do your job: the skills needed for a task and the know-how to use them productively and efficiently.

These *technical skills* are mandatory if you want to land a job within your profession. *Technical skills*, while transferable, vary from profession to profession, so many of your current *technical skills* will only be transferable within your current profession.

2. *Transferable Skills That Apply in All Professions*

These are the skills that underlie your ability to execute the responsibilities of your job effectively, whatever that job may be. They are the foundation of all the professional success you will experience in this or any other career you may pursue over the years.

Transferable Skills and Professional Values

Here are the *transferable skills* and *professional values* that will speed the conclusion of this job search and your ongoing professional success. You'll find that you already have some of them to a greater or lesser degree, and if you are committed to making a success of your life, you'll commit to further development of all of them.

Transferable Skills	Professional Values
Technical	*Motivation and Energy*
Critical Thinking	*Commitment and Reliability*
Communication	*Determination*
Multitasking	*Pride and Integrity*
Creativity	*Productivity*
Teamwork	*Systems and Procedures*
Leadership	

As you read about each *transferable skill* and *professional value* you may, for example, read about *communication*, and think, "Yes, I can see how communication skills are important in all jobs and at all levels of the promotional ladder, and, hallelujah, I have good communication skills." When this happens, take the time to recall examples of the role each different *communication skill* (there are eight of them) plays in each of your work responsibilities.

You will also realize that there are skills that need more work. Whenever you identify a *transferable skill* that needs work, you have found a *professional development project*: improving that skill. Your attention to these areas will repay you for the rest of your working life, no matter how you make a living.

Transferable Skills
TECHNICAL SKILLS
The *technical skills* of your job are the foundation of success within your current profession; without them you won't even land a job, much less keep it for long or win a promotion. They speak to your *ability* to

do the job, those essential skills necessary for the day-to-day execution of your duties. These *technical skills* vary from profession to profession and do not refer to anything technical *as such* or to technology.

However, it is a given that one of the *technical skills* essential to every job is technological competence. You must be proficient in all the technology and Internet-based applications relevant to your work. Even when you are not working in a technology field, strong *technology skills* will enhance your stability and help you leverage professional growth.

Some of your technology skills will only be relevant within your current profession, while others (Word, Excel, PowerPoint, to name the obvious) will be transferable across all industry and professional lines. Staying current with the essential *technical* and *technology skills* of your chosen career path is the keystone of your professional stability and growth.

CRITICAL THINKING SKILLS

As I noted in the previous chapter, your job, whatever it is, exists to solve problems and to prevent problems from arising within your area of expertise. *Critical thinking, analytical,* or *problem-solving skills* represent a systematic approach to dealing with the challenges presented by your work. *Critical thinking skills* allow you to think through a problem, define the challenge and its possible solutions, and then evaluate and implement the best solution from all available options.

Fifty percent of the success of any project is in the preparation; *critical thinking* is at the heart of that preparation. In addition, using *critical thinking* to properly define a problem always leads to a better solution.

COMMUNICATION SKILLS

As George Bernard Shaw said: "The greatest problem in communication is the illusion that it has been accomplished." Every professional job today demands good *communication skills*, but what are they?

When the professional world talks about *communication skills*, it isn't just referring to verbal communication, but to four primary skills and four supportive communication skills. The primary *communication skills* are:

- Verbal skills—what you say and how you say it.
- Listening skills—listening to understand, rather than just waiting your turn to talk.
- Writing skills—clear written communication creates a lasting impression of who you are and is essential for success in any professional career.
- Technological communication skills—your ability to evaluate the protocols, strengths, and weaknesses of alternative communication media, and then choose the medium appropriate to your audience and message.

The four supportive *communication skills* are:

- Grooming and dress—these tell others who you are and how you feel about yourself.
- Social graces—how you behave toward others in all situations; this defines your professionalism.
- Body language—this displays how you're feeling deep inside, a form of communication that predates speech. For truly effective communication, what your mouth says must be in harmony with what your body says.
- Emotional IQ—your emotional self-awareness, your maturity in dealing with others in the full range of human interaction.

All the transferable skills are interconnected—for example, good *verbal skills* require both *listening* and *critical thinking skills* to accurately process incoming information and enable you to present your outgoing verbal messaging persuasively in light of the interests and sophistication of your audience so that it is understood and accepted. Develop effective skills in all eight of the subsets that together comprise *communication skills* and you'll gain enormous control over what you can achieve, how you are perceived, and what happens in your life.

MULTITASKING

This is one of the most desirable skills of the new era. According to numerous studies, however, the *multitasking* demands of modern professional life are causing massive frustration and meltdowns for professionals everywhere. The problem is *not multitasking*, the problem is the assumption that *multitasking* means being reactive to *all* incoming stimuli and therefore jumping around from one task to another as the emergency of the moment dictates. Such a definition of *multitasking* would of course leave you feeling like wild horses are attached to your extremities and tearing you limb from limb.

Few people understand what *multitasking* abilities are built on: sound *time management* and *organizational* skills. Here are the basics:

Establish Priorities

Multitasking is based on three things:

1. Being organized
2. Establishing priorities
3. Managing your time

The Plan, Do, Review Cycle

At the end of every day, review what you've accomplished:

• What happened: A.M. and P.M.?
• What went well? Do more of it.
• What went wrong? How do I fix it?
• What projects do I need to move forward tomorrow?
• Rank each project. A = Must be completed tomorrow. B = Good to be completed tomorrow. C = If there is spare time from A and B priorities.
• Make a prioritized To Do list.
• Stick to it.

Doing this at the end of the day keeps you informed about what you have achieved, and lets you know that you have invested your time in the most important activities today and will tomorrow, so you feel better, sleep better, and come in tomorrow focused and ready to rock.

TEAMWORK

Companies depend on teams because the professional world revolves around the complex challenges of making money, and such complexities require teams of people to provide ongoing solutions. This means that you must work efficiently and respectfully with other people who have totally different responsibilities, backgrounds, objectives, and areas of expertise. It's true that individual initiative is important, but as a professional, much of the really important work you do will be done as a member of a group. Your long-term stability and success require that you learn the arts of cooperation, team-based decision-making, and team communication.

Teamwork demands that a commitment to the team and its success comes first. This means you take on a task because it needs to be done, not because it makes you look good.

As a team player you:

- Always cooperate.
- Always make decisions based on team goals.
- Always keep team members informed.
- Always keep commitments.
- Always share credit, never blame.

If you become a successful leader in your professional life, it's a given that you were first a reliable team player, because a leader must understand the dynamics of teamwork before she can leverage them. When teamwork is coupled with the other *transferable skills* and *professional values, it results in greater responsibility and promotions.*

LEADERSHIP SKILLS

Leadership is the most complex of all the *transferable skills* and combines all the others. As you develop *teamwork skills*, notice how you are willing to follow true leaders, but don't fall in line with people who don't respect you and who don't have your best interests at heart. When others believe in your competence, and believe you have everyone's success as your goal, they will follow you. When your actions inspire others to think more, learn more, do more, and become more, you are becoming a leader. This will ultimately be recognized and rewarded with promotion into and up the ranks of management.

- Your job as a leader is to help your team succeed, and your *teamwork skills* give you the smarts to pull a team together as a cohesive unit.
- Your *technical* expertise, *critical thinking*, and *creativity skills* help you correctly define the challenges your team faces, and give you the wisdom to guide them toward solutions.
- Your *communication skills* enable your team to *buy into* your directives and goals. There's nothing more demoralizing than a leader who can't clearly articulate why you're doing what you're doing.
- Your *creativity* (discussed next) comes from the wide frame of reference you have for your work and the profession and industry in which you work, enabling you to come up with solutions that others might not have seen.
- Your *multitasking skills*, based on sound *time management* and *organizational* abilities, enable you to create a practical blueprint for success and your team to take ownership of the task and deliver the expected results on time.

Leadership is a combination and outgrowth of all the *transferable skills* plus the clear presence of all the *professional values* we are about to discuss. Leaders aren't born; they are self-made. And just like anything else, it takes hard work.

CREATIVITY

Your creativity comes from the frame of reference you have for your work, profession, and industry. This wide frame of reference enables you to see the *patterns* that lie behind challenges, and so connect the dots and come up with solutions that others might have missed because they were mired in details and didn't have that holistic frame of reference that enabled them to step back and view the issue in its larger context.

There's a big difference between *creativity* and just having ideas. Ideas are like headaches: We all get them once in a while, and like headaches, they disappear as mysteriously as they arrived. *Creativity*, on the other hand, is the ability to develop those ideas with the strategic and tactical know-how that brings them to life. Someone is seen as creative when his ideas produce tangible results. *Creativity* also demands that you harness other transferable skills to bring those ideas to life. *Creativity* springs from:

- Your *critical thinking skills*, applied within an area of *technical expertise* (an area where your *technical skills* give you a frame of reference for what works and what doesn't).
- Your *multitasking skills*, which in combination with your *critical thinking* and *technical skills* allow you to break your challenge down into specific steps and determine which approach is best.
- Your *communication skills*, which allow you to explain your approach persuasively to your target audience.
- Your *teamwork* and *leadership skills*, which enable you to enlist others and bring the idea to fruition.

Professional Values

Professional values are an interconnected set of core beliefs that enable professionals to determine the right judgment call in any given situation. Highly prized by employers, this value system is integral to the *transferable skills*.

MOTIVATION AND ENERGY

Motivation and *energy* express themselves in your engagement with and enthusiasm for your work and profession. They involve an eagerness to learn and grow professionally, and a willingness to take the rough with the smooth in pursuit of meaningful goals. *Motivation* is invariably expressed by the *energy* you demonstrate in your work. You always give that extra effort to get the job done and get it done right.

COMMITMENT AND RELIABILITY

This means dedication to your profession, and the empowerment that comes from knowing how your part contributes to the whole. Your *commitment* expresses itself in your *reliability*. The *committed* professional is willing to do whatever it takes to get a job done, whenever and for however long it takes to get the job done, even if that includes duties that might not appear in a job description and that might be perceived by less enlightened colleagues as beneath them.

DETERMINATION

The *determination* you display with the travails of your work speaks of a resilient professional who does not back off when a problem or situation gets tough. It's a *professional value* that marks you as someone who chooses to be part of the solution.

The *determined* professional has decided to make a difference with her presence every day, because it is the *right* thing to do, and because it makes the time go faster.

She is willing to do whatever it takes to get a job done, and she will demonstrate that determination on behalf of colleagues who share the same values.

PRIDE AND INTEGRITY

If a job's worth doing, it's worth doing right. That's what *pride* in your work really means: attention to detail and a *commitment* to doing your very best. *Integrity* applies to all your dealings, whether with coworkers, management, customers, or vendors. Honesty really *is* the best policy.

PRODUCTIVITY

Always working toward *productivity* in your areas of responsibility, through efficiencies of time, resources, money, and effort.

ECONOMY

Remember the word "frugal"? It doesn't mean miserliness. It means making the most of what you've got, using everything with the greatest efficiency. Companies that know how to be frugal with their resources will prosper in good times and bad, and if you know how to be frugal, you'll do the same.

SYSTEMS AND PROCEDURES

This is a natural outgrowth of all the other *transferable skills* and *professional values*. Your *commitment* to your profession in all these ways gives you an appreciation of the need for *systems and procedures* and their implementation only after careful thought. You understand and always follow the chain of command. You don't implement your own "improved" procedures or encourage others to do so. If ways of doing things don't make sense or are interfering with efficiency and profitability, you work through the system to get them changed.

How Transferable Skills and Professional Values Impact Your Job Search

Development of *transferable skills* and *professional values* will be repaid with job offers, better job security, and improved professional horizons. When you are seen to embody these *transferable skills* and *professional values* in your work and in the ways you interact with the people in your professional world, you will become known and respected as a consummate professional, and this can dramatically differentiate your candidacy.

For example, think through how a job-posting requirement for, say, "good communication skills" applies to your work. It probably used to make you think of verbal skills, but now you know that employers think of *communication skills* as a web of eight connected and supporting skills.

In the next chapter, we'll look at what you're selling and what your customers are buying, and part of that conversation involves integrating each of these *transferable skills* and *professional values* into every responsibility and deliverable of your daily work. When you can talk to interviewers about your work in ways that highlight your application of these skills, you will be one big step closer to turning interviews into offers and succeeding on the job.

CHAPTER 3

UNDERSTAND WHAT YOU'RE SELLING AND WHAT YOUR CUSTOMERS ARE BUYING

IN THE PREVIOUS TWO CHAPTERS, you learned about the criteria employers use to make smart hiring decisions, and it should be clear by now that having a deep understanding of your work and its role within the department and in the larger goals of the corporation will make you a more desirable candidate.

The better the understanding you develop of the real guts of your target job, the better your performance will be at the job interview. Just because you've done the same work for years doesn't mean you necessarily understand how employers are thinking about and prioritizing its deliverables, or how they are expressing and making hiring decisions based on those needs.

You might recall that all your earliest and most important business lessons revolved around "getting to know your customer," "the customer is always right," and "selling to the customer's needs." In job transitions, you are a salesperson selling a product that happens to be the *professional you,* and so you need to get inside your customers' heads and learn what it is they want to buy this season. This is the key to understanding how you can best package your background and skills.

There's a practical and easy way to do this, and it's called a Target Job Deconstruction (TJD). TJD is the best way to get a tight focus on what your customers are buying and what you have to sell. Your investment in TJD will yield an understanding of:

- How employers prioritize their needs for this job
- The words employers use to express their needs
- The skills you bring to every need
- Where the focus will be during interviews
- The interview questions that will be heading your way and why
- The challenges associated with each aspect of the job
- How you handle the challenges associated with each aspect of the job
- Relevant examples with which to illustrate your answers
- A behavioral profile for getting hired and for ongoing professional success
- A behavioral profile for *not* getting hired and for ongoing professional *failure*

Oh, and if that's not enough, doing a TJD can also supercharge your resume by giving you a template for the story your resume *must* tell to be successful—see the latest edition of *Knock 'em Dead Resumes* for more. Invest in your success with TJD: It's simple to do and the results can be magical.

Target Job Deconstruction: The Way Into Your Customer's Head

Step #1: Collect Postings

Collect 6–10 job postings for the job you are best qualified to do and save them in a folder (digital and hard copy). The location of the job doesn't matter; what's important is how employers are *prioritizing* and *expressing* their needs.

Not sure where to start? Try these job aggregators (or spiders, robots, or bots) that run around thousands of job sites looking for jobs with your chosen keywords:

www.indeed.com
www.simplyhired.com
www.WorkTree.com
www.JobBankUSA.com
www.Job-Search-Engine.com
www.JobSniper.com
www.SourceTool.com
www.jobster.com

Step #2: Define a Target Job Title

Open a new Microsoft Word document and save it as "TJD."

Add a subhead reading *Job Title*, then copy and paste in the variations from each of your sample job descriptions. Looking at the result, you can say, "When employers are hiring people like *me*, they tend to describe the job title with these words."

You can use this information to come up with a *Target Job Title* for your resume. Most resumes don't actually list Target Job Titles, but if you add one, it can help the reader immediately establish who and what the resume is about. As you will be taking copies of your resume to job interviews, this simple step positions your candidacy appropriately from the moment you sit down with an interviewer.

Step #3: Prioritize Employer Needs

Now, add a second subhead titled:

Skills/Responsibilities/Experience/Deliverables

Look through the job postings for a *single requirement* that's common to all of your job postings. Take the most complete description of that *single requirement* and copy and paste it into your TJD doc, putting a (6) by your entry to signify that it is common to all job descriptions. For example, an accountant might make this entry:

(6) Eight years' accounts payable experience required, ideally in high-volume insurance office.

Add any other words and phrases from the other job postings used to describe this same area to the bottom of the entry. Repeat this exercise for other requirements common to all of your sample job postings.

A Word of Caution

Hiring managers hire candidates based on credentials, not potential. When doing a TJD, you might come across skills that you don't have: "Everyone's looking for six sigma and lean management skills and I don't even know what those words mean." As a rule of thumb, and especially in a tight job market when competition is fierce, you need about 70 percent of a job's requirements to pursue that job with reasonable hope of landing interviews and a job offer. If you complete the TJD process and realize you don't make the grade, you have probably saved yourself a good deal of frustration pursuing a job you had no real chance of landing. What you need to do in this instance is pull your title goals back one level and pursue a job where you have the majority of the required skills. Then you can subsequently use this TJD and the missing skills it identifies as a professional development tool: You'll need to develop those skills to warrant a promotion.

Step #4: Complete Skill Analysis

Repeat the process from Step #3 for requirements common to five of the jobs, then four, and so on all the way down to those requirements mentioned in only one job posting.

When this is done, you can look at your work and say, "when employers are hiring people like *me,* they":

- Refer to them by these job titles
- Prioritize their needs in *this* way
- Use *these* words to describe their prioritized needs

Step #5: Identify the Problem Prevention and Solution Issues

Jobs are only ever added to the payroll to make or save money for the company, or to otherwise increase productivity.

All jobs, yours included, achieve this by *identifying, preventing, and solving* the problems that occur in your area of expertise every day, problems that interfere with the pursuit of helping the company maintain profitability.

Every requirement of your target job is related to this profit imperative in some way. Starting with those requirements common to all of your job description samples, identify the problems that typically arise when you are executing your duties in this area. Then for each problem identify:

- How you execute your responsibilities to prevent this problem from arising in the first place
- How you tackle such a situation when it does occur, with examples

When we apply the problem prevention and solution issues to our example from earlier—"Eight years' accounts payable experience required, ideally in high-volume insurance office"—you begin to see the value of this project.

The "Eight years' experience" becomes less valuable than what you have learned to do in those years. An accountant's job is primarily concerned with protecting cash flow, so if this were your target job, you would be thinking about:

- The ways you execute your duties to prevent accounts payable going over thirty days.
- What you do with thirty-day accounts to get the money in, and what you do to prevent these accounts going to sixty days delinquent; and so on.

This not only gets you consciously thinking about the real guts of your work, it gives you ammunition to use in job interviews to position yourself as an altogether different candidate.

Step #6: A Behavioral Profile for Success

Revisit each individual requirement and recall the *best* person you have ever known doing that aspect of the job. Identify specifically what made that person stand out in your mind as a true professional. Continuing with our example, your entry might now look like this:

(6) Eight years' accounts payable experience required, ideally in high-volume insurance office

Excel, accounting software, Peachtree, problem accounts

Problem prevention and solution examples:

(Habits to prevent collections problems)

(Habitual solutions for collections problems)

Success profile:

Angela Ciccine. Well-dressed and groomed. Great problem-solving skills, listens well, smiles, supportive, team player, great organizational and time-management skills. Firm when she needs to be.

You then repeat this little exercise for every itemized requirement you identified in the TJD process. This will give you a behavioral profile of the person every employer wants to hire, and a behavioral blueprint for subsequent professional success.

Step #7: A Behavioral Profile for Failure

The last step of the TJD is to ensure that you are not doing anything to inadvertently sabotage your candidacy or success on future jobs. Revisit each individual requirement one last time and recall the *worst* person you have ever known doing that aspect of the job. Your entry for that first requirement will now look something like this:

(6) Eight years' accounts payable experience required, ideally in high volume insurance office

Excel, accounting software, Peachtree, problem accounts

Problem prevention and solution examples:

(Habits to prevent collections problems)

(Habitual solutions for collections problems)

Success profile:

Angela Ciccine. Well-dressed and groomed. Great problem-solving skills, listens well, smiles, supportive, team player, great organizational and time-management skills. Firm when she needs to be.

Failure profile:

Jerome Mulhallan. Passive aggressive; never listened, poor communications, never on time with projects or for meetings, never smiled, critical, no manners.

Then repeat this for the other itemized requirement you identified in the TJD process and you will have a complete behavioral profile of the person no employer wants to hire and a behavioral blueprint for professional failure.

Putting It All Together

This TJD process also tells you what your interviewers will be asking about. You know how employers prioritize their needs for your job, and you have thought through the issues that complicate your job every day. You have examples of the ways you execute your duties to prevent typical problems from arising, and you have examples of you tackling the problems that everyone in your job has to face every week. You understand the behavioral profile of the person employers want to hire and the profile of the person they want to avoid at all costs.

Armed with the TJD and your understanding of the *transferable skills*, *professional values*, and secrets of the hire, you can now dive into the interview process with confidence in your product. We'll start with the telephone interview, a frequent screening tool.

CHAPTER 4

HOW TO ACE
THE TELEPHONE INTERVIEW

LITTLE HAPPENS IN THE PROFESSIONAL WORLD WITHOUT CONVERSA-TIONS taking place; that is why the focus of your job search should always be to *get into conversations with the people who can hire you as quickly and as often as possible.*

Your first conversation will usually be over the telephone; that conversation may be planned, but it might also happen unexpectedly.

Employers use the telephone as a time-management tool. It is quicker and easier to weed out candidates on the telephone than in person. On the other hand, your goal is to turn a telephone interview into a face-to-face meeting, so you need to convince the interviewer that he will not be wasting time in meeting with you in person.

The Phone Can Ring When You Least Expect It

Telephone interviews happen in one of three ways:

- You have arranged a specific time for a telephone interview.
- An employer calls unexpectedly as the result of a resume you have mailed or e-mailed.

- You are making a marketing or networking call, and the recruiter or hiring manager goes straight into a formal screening process because you have aroused her interest.

Now, this book is about the verbal interactions between you and the interviewer and we simply don't have the space to address the activities that lead to telephone interviews; however, you will find a comprehensive discussion of how to make marketing and networking calls in the very latest *Knock 'em Dead: The Ultimate Job Search Guide*.

Odds are that you will experience plenty of telephone interviews during your job search. No matter how that conversation happens, you must always be prepared to think and act clearly, so that you can turn the call into a face-to-face meeting.

Perhaps the most important consideration with a telephone interview is that the employer can only judge you with his ears. With that in mind:

- If the call comes unexpectedly, and screaming kids or barking dogs surround you, stay calm and sound positive, friendly, and collected: "Thank you for calling, Mr. Wooster. Would you wait a moment while I close the door?" You can then take a minute to calm yourself, pull up the company website on your screen, and get your paperwork organized without causing offense.
- If you need to move to another phone, say so. Otherwise, put the caller on hold, take a few controlled, deep breaths to slow down your pounding heart, put a smile on your face (it improves the timbre of your voice), and pick up the phone again. Now you are in control of yourself and the situation.
- If you are heading out the door for an interview, or if some other emergency makes this a bad time for an unexpected incoming call, say so straight away and reschedule: "I'm heading out the door for an appointment, Ms. Bassett. Can we schedule a time when I can call you back?" Beware of overfamiliarity: You should always refer to the interviewer by his surname until invited to do otherwise.

In the course of the 200 telephone interviews a year that I average (they are radio interviews, not job interviews, but I'm sure you can appreciate the similar level of nervous tension), I've found that standing for the interview calms my adrenaline rush a little, helps my breathing, and allows me to sound confident and relaxed. It might work for you, too, so give it a try.

The Telephone Interview Begins

However your conversation with the headhunter, corporate recruiter, or hiring manager comes to pass, after a few introductory words on either side, the questions will begin and there's a good chance the first one will be:

Tell me a little about yourself.

There's logic behind the question; it is not an invitation to ramble. The interviewer wants to know about your experience and qualifications for this job and if they warrant bringing you in for a face-to-face meeting. Answer the question well and you create a good first impression and set the tone for your candidacy; you also immediately feel more confident.

As it turns out, you already have the answer to this question pretty much prepared. The TJD exercise helped you identify:

- Exactly how employers prioritize, think about, and express the responsibilities of the job
- The way your job fits into and contributes to company goals
- The problems your job is there to identify, prevent, and solve
- The ways you execute your responsibilities to identify and prevent problems from arising
- The ways you handle problems when they do arise

If you've read *Knock 'em Dead Resumes,* you will already have applied this unique approach to developing a killer resume, and you will have a Performance Profile at the top of your resume that gives a succinct portrait of the relevant skills you bring to the table.

If you haven't used *Knock 'em Dead Resumes* yet, take the four or five most common employer requirements from your TJD and turn them into four or five sentences reflecting your experience in each of those areas. This gives you a condensed professional work history that focuses on the experience most important to employers looking to hire for this position. Add chronology—"I spent_____years at _____ and this is where I learned . . ."—and you'll show the professional development that brought you to the point you are at today.

This isn't a question that you can answer effectively without thought and preparation, so you'll need to take a little time to think about your experiences to date, comparing them to the major requirements identified in your TJD and understanding how they have prepared you for this job. For example:

"I'm the area director of marketing for the_____metropolitan area. I oversee all aspects of marketing to acquire and retain basic, digital, and online customers through tactics such as mass media and direct mail. In addition, I launch new products/services like VOI. I have a team of forty-six employees, which also includes twenty-six door-to-door sales reps.

"I rose to this position over fifteen years, climbing through the ranks based on my performance, achievement, and an ever-growing frame of reference for my profession and our business. As we get into the nuts-and-bolts discussion of the job, I hope to show you that I have a real understanding of the challenges faced by my direct reports, a steady hand, and the managerial skills required for a motivated and productive department."

This question is often followed by another:

What do you know about the company?

The interviewer spends the majority of her waking hours in the environment that the winning candidate will join. Your knowledge of the job and the company is a piece of the jigsaw puzzle that helps her evaluate your enthusiasm and *motivation* for your work. If you don't understand what the company does and is known for, you will lose out to candidates who do.

Use the Internet, company website, and networking contacts to gain insight into the company, its products, and why it is a good place to work. Visit the company website and read media coverage on the company and its key executives (via Google News, for example), as well as general news about the issues affecting your industry. Your research will raise as many questions as it answers, and you can use this in your answer: "I read that _____ , and wonder how this is affecting you . . . ?" Such questions demonstrate engagement with your profession and get the interviewer talking, perhaps giving you useful information. It's okay to throw in some relevant personal details as well, such as the fact that working for the company will bring you closer to family.

The company representative may talk about the corporation, and from your research or the website on your screen you may also know something about the outfit. A little flattery goes a long way: Admire a company's achievements when you can, and by inference you admire the interviewer. Likewise, if any areas of common interest arise, comment on them, and agree with the interviewer when reasonably possible—people usually hire people like themselves.

The Questions Start Flowing

After learning a little bit about your professional background and what you know about the company, the questions will start to flow in earnest.

After your response to a couple of initial questions, there will likely be a silence on the other end of the line. Be patient; the interviewer may need a few seconds to digest your words. When the interviewer is interested, you will be asked a question; when the interviewer has a problem with what you have said, you'll face an objection. We'll handle what to do in both situations.

Any question means the listener is interested: This is known as a "buy signal." Questions you might expect include:

How much experience do you have?

Too much or too little experience could easily rule you out. Be careful how you answer this question and try to gain time. It is a vague question, and you have a right to ask for qualifications. Employers typically define jobs by years of experience. At the same time, there is currently a major move away from simple chronological experience toward the more important concern about what you can deliver on the job. Managers and HR pros are now more open to thinking in terms of "performance requirements" and "deliverables" than ever before.

Here are a couple of ways to handle it:

"I have _____ years' chronological experience, but if you could you give me a brief outline of the performance requirements, I can give you a more accurate answer." Then with the information you might be able to answer, "I am comfortable with all aspects of the pre-sales, sales, and post-sales process and have considerable experience, comfort, and contacts throughout the B-to-B community here in Pittsburgh, including public corporations, institutions, and start-ups."

Or:

"Could you help me with that question? If you give me a brief outline of the performance requirements, I can give you a more accurate answer." Or, "I have _____ years' experience, but they aren't necessarily typical. If you'd give me a few details on the performance requirements I'd be able to give you a more accurate answer."

The employer's response, while gaining you time, tells you what it takes to do the job and therefore what aspects of your experience are most relevant. Take mental notes as the employer talks—you can even write them down if you have time. Then give an appropriate response.

You can move the conversation forward by asking a follow-up question of your own. For example: "The areas of expertise you require sound like a match to my experience, and it sounds as if you have some exciting projects at hand. What projects would I be involved with in the first few months?"

The next question might be something like:

Do you have a degree?

An easy question if you have one. If not, qualify your answer and point the way forward: "My education was cut short by the necessity of earning a living. However, I'm currently enrolled in classes to complete my degree." If you don't have a degree and an objection is raised, you'll see how to handle it in a few pages.

Buy Signal: How much are you making/do you want?

This is a direct question looking for a direct answer, yet it is a knockout question, so you should proceed warily. Earning either too little or too much could ruin your chances before you're given the opportunity to shine in person. There are a number of options that could serve you better than a direct answer. First, you must understand that questions about money at this point in the conversation are being used to screen you in or screen you out. The answers you give now should be geared toward getting you in the door and into a face-to-face meeting. (The serious issues of salary and salary negotiations are handled in the negotiation chapter.) For now, just know the main options are as follows:

- **Direct answer:** If you know the salary range for the position and there is a fit, give a straightforward answer.
- **Indirect answer:** "In the 50s." Or "in the 120s."

- **Give a range.** Come up with two figures: a fair offer considering your experience and job location, and a great offer considering your experience and job location: "Hopefully between $x and $y. What's most important is an opportunity to make a difference. If I am the right person for the job, I'm sure you'll make me a fair offer. By the way, what is the salary range for this position?"
- **Put yourself above the money:** "I'm looking for an opportunity that will give me the opportunity to make a difference with my efforts. If I am the right person for the job, I'm sure you'll make me a fair offer. By the way, what is the salary range for this position?"

When you give a salary range rather than a single figure, you have more flexibility and have greater chance of "clicking" with the employer's approved range for the position.

In the unlikely event that you are pressed for an exact dollar figure at this point—and if you have the skills for the job, and you are concerned that your current low salary will eliminate you—you might add, "I realize this is well below industry norms, but it does not reflect on my expertise or experience in any way. It speaks of the need for me to make a strategic career move to where I can be compensated competitively and based on my skills and accomplishments."

How to Deal with Objections

By no means will every telephone interview consist of a few simple questions and then an invitation to interview. Sometimes the interviewer will have objections to your candidacy. This usually comes in the form of a statement, not a question: "Send me a resume," or "I don't have time to see you," or "You are earning too much," or "You'll have to talk to personnel," or "I don't need anyone like you right now." These seem like brush-off lines, but they can often be turned into interviews.

In dealing with objections, nothing is gained by confrontation, while much can be gained by an appreciation of the other's viewpoint.

Consequently, most objections you hear are best har
demonstrating your understanding of the other's viewpoin.
responses with phrases like "I understand," or "I can appreciate your
position," or "I see your point," or "Of course." Follow up with statements
like "However," or "Also consider," or a similar line that allows the
opportunity for rebuttal and gathering of further information.

Notice that all the following suggested response models end
with a question, one that helps you learn more about the reason for
the objection, which in turn helps you overcome it and move the
conversation in the direction of a meeting.

It's not necessary to memorize these responses verbatim, only to
understand the underlying concept and then put together responses in
words that are natural to your personality and style of speech.

Why don't you send me a resume?

The employer may be genuinely interested in seeing your resume as
a first step in the interview cycle, or it may be a polite way of getting
you off the phone. You should identify the real reason without causing
antagonism, and at the same time open up the conversation. A good
reply would be, "Of course, Mr. Grant. Would you give me your exact
title and your e-mail address? Thank you. So that I can be sure that
my qualifications fit your needs, what skills are you looking for in this
position?" or "What specific job title and opening should I refer to
when I send it?"

Notice the steps:

- Agreement with the prospective employer
- A demonstration of understanding
- A question to further the conversation (in this instance to confirm
  that an opening actually exists)

Answering in this fashion will open up the conversation. Mr. Grant
will relay the aspects of the job that are important to him, and you can
use the additional information to move the conversation forward again

with new information about your experience. Following Mr. Grant's response, you can recap the match between his needs and your skills:

"Assuming my resume matches your needs, as I am confident that it will, could we pencil in a date and time for an interview next week? I am available next Thursday and Friday; which would be preferable to you?"

A penciled-in date and time for an interview very rarely gets canceled, because they don't actually get "penciled in"—in this electronic age, they immediately take up a time slot in the schedule.

I don't have time to see you.

If the employer is too busy to see you, it indicates that she has work pressures, and by recognizing that, you can show yourself as the one to alleviate some of those pressures with your problem-solving skills. You should avoid confrontation, however; it is important that you demonstrate empathy for the person with whom you are speaking. Agree, empathize, and ask a question that moves the conversation forward:

"I understand how busy you must be; it sounds like a competent, dedicated, and efficient _____ could be of some assistance. Perhaps I could call you back at a better time to discuss how I might make a contribution in easing the pressure at peak times. When are you least busy, in the morning or afternoon?"

The interviewer will either make time to talk now or arrange a better time for the two of you to talk further.

You could also try, "Since you are so busy, what is the best time of day for you? First thing in the morning, or is the afternoon a quieter time?" Or you could suggest, "If you would like to see my resume, you could study my background at your leisure. What's your e-mail address? Thanks. What would be a good time of day to follow up on this?"

You are earning too much.

Don't give up immediately; follow the process through: "Oh, I'm sorry to hear that—what is the range for that position?" Depending on the degree of salary discrepancy, you might reiterate your interest.

If your current earnings are higher than the approved range, you could say, "Mr. Smith, my current employers feel I am well worth the money I earn due to my skills, dedication, and honesty. When we meet, I'm sure I can convince you of my ability to contribute to your department. A meeting would provide an opportunity to make that evaluation, wouldn't it?"

If the job really doesn't pay enough—and there will be openings for which you are earning too much—you've gotten "close, but no cigar!" You can also refer to the negotiation chapter later in the book, where you will find further advice on dealing with this issue.

We only promote from within.

Your response could be, "[smiling] Your development of employees is a major reason I want to get in! I am bright, conscientious, and motivated. When you do hire from the outside, and it must happen on occasion, what do you look for?" or "How do I get into consideration for such opportunities?"

The response finishes with a question designed to carry the conversation forward and to give you a new opportunity to sell yourself. Notice that the response logically presupposes that the company does hire from the outside, as all companies obviously do, despite your being told otherwise.

You'll have to talk to Human Resources.

In this case, you reply, "Of course, Mr. Grant. Whom should I speak to in HR, and what specific position should I mention?"

You cover a good deal of ground with that response. You establish whether there is a job there or whether you are being fobbed off on HR to waste their time and your own. Also, you move the conversation forward again while modifying it to your advantage. Develop a specific job-related question to ask while the employer is answering the first question. It can open a fruitful line for you to pursue. If you receive a nonspecific reply, probe a little deeper. A simple phrase like, "That's interesting. Please tell me more," or "Why's that?" will usually do the trick.

Or you can ask, "When I speak to HR, will it be about a specific job you have, or is it to see whether I might fill a position elsewhere in the company?"

Armed with the resulting information, you can talk to HR about your conversation with Mr. Grant. Remember to get the name of a specific person in HR with whom to speak, and quote this prior contact by name in any e-mail or verbal contact:

"Good morning, Ms. Johnson. Cary Grant, over in marketing, suggested we should speak to arrange an interview for the sales associate position." This way you show HR that you are not a time-waster, because you have already spoken to the person who is hiring for this job.

Don't look at the HR department as a roadblock. It may contain a host of opportunities for you. In many companies, different departments could use your talents, and HR is probably the only department that knows about all the openings. With larger companies, you might be able to arrange interviews for two or three different positions!

I really wanted someone with a degree.

"Mr. Smith, I appreciate your viewpoint. It was necessary that I start earning a living early in life, because of _____ (the needs dictated by your circumstances). That said, I have used my employment as on-the-job training and believe my skills, knowledge, and judgment are the equal of any candidate you are likely to interview, degreed or not. If we meet, I am certain you will recognize the value of my practical experience."

If you have been smart enough to enroll in a course or two in order to pursue that always-important degree, you can finish your response with, "I should also add that I am currently enrolled in courses to complete

- "Would it be of value if I described my experience in _____ ?"
- "Then my experience in _____ should be a great help to you."
- "I recently completed an _____ project just like that. Would it be relevant to discuss it?"

When you identify an employer's imminent challenges and demonstrate how your skills can lessen the load, you portray yourself as a properly focused employee with a problem-solving attitude, and immediately move closer to a face-to-face interview, because managers want to hire a problem-solver who knows the job.

How to Use Verbal Signals of Agreement and Understanding

You can also keep up your end of the conversation by giving verbal signals that you are engaged in what is being said. You do this with occasional short interjections that don't interrupt the employer's flow but let him know you are paying attention. Comments like "uh-huh," "that's interesting," "okay," "great," and "yes, yes," are verbal equivalents of the body language techniques we'll discuss further on.

Practical Considerations of Using the Telephone

Always speak directly into the telephone, with the mouthpiece about one inch from your mouth. Numbered among the mystical properties of telephone technology is its excellence at amplifying background noise. This is excelled only by its power to transmit the sounds of food and gum being chewed, or smoke being inhaled and exhaled. Smokers take note: Nonsmokers instinctively discriminate, and they will assume that even if you don't actually light up at the interview, you'll have been chain-smoking beforehand and will carry the smell with you as long as you're around. They probably won't even give you a chance to get through the door once they hear you puffing away over the phone.

Understanding someone over the telephone can sometimes be a challenge, so if you didn't hear or didn't understand a question, ask the speaker to repeat it. If you need time to think about your answer—and that is quite acceptable—say so: "Let me think about that for a moment."

You should take notes when possible; they will be invaluable if the employer is interrupted. You can jot down the topic under discussion, then when she gets back on the line, helpfully recap: "We were just discussing . . ." This will be appreciated and show that you are organized and paying attention. Your notes will also help you prepare for the face-to-face meeting.

Asking about Money and Benefits

Under no circumstances should you ask about salary or benefits and vacation time; that comes much later. Your single objective at this point is to meet face-to-face; money is not an issue. If the interviewer brings up a direct question about how much you are earning, you can't get around it, so be honest. On the other hand, if you are asked how much you want, answer truthfully that at this point you don't know enough about the company or the job to answer that question. There is a whole chapter later in the book that covers negotiation in some detail.

Ask for the Face-to-Face Meeting

The telephone interview has come to an end when you are asked whether you have any questions. This is a wind-down question, so it is a good opening to get some specific questions of your own answered that can advance your candidacy. If you haven't asked them already, be sure to ask the questions we addressed previously under the heading, "Conversation Is a Two-Way Street." The answers you get to these questions will give you the ammunition to make a powerful summation, win the face-to-face, and help you prepare for that interview.

If you have not already asked or been invited to meet the interviewer, now is the time to take the initiative. Your last question goes something like this, "It sounds like a very interesting opportunity, Ms. Bassett, and a situation where I could definitely make a contribution. The most pressing question I have now is when can we schedule a meeting?"

When You Score an In-Person Interview

When an invitation for an interview is extended, there are practical matters that you need to clarify, like the date and time and where the interview will take place; don't assume it's at a facility that you associate with the company. You will also want to inquire about the interview procedure:

- "How many interviews typically occur before a decision is made?"
- "Who else will be part of the selection process, and what are their roles within the department or company?"
- "What is the timeframe for filling this position, and how many other people are in consideration at this time?"

Ask about the direction the interview will take: "Would you tell me some of the areas we will address on Thursday?" Or "What do you hope to learn about me on Thursday?" The knowledge gained will help you prepare, and will allow you time to bone up on any weak or rusty areas. This is also a good time to establish how long the meeting is expected to last, which will give you some idea of how to pace yourself.

No matter how many questions you get answered in this initial conversation, there will always be something you forgot, so ask: "If I need any additional information before the interview, may I feel free to get back to you?" The interviewer will naturally agree. This allows you to call again to satisfy any curiosity—and it will also enable you to increase rapport. Don't take too much advantage of it, though: One well-placed phone call that contains two or three considered questions will be appreciated; four or five phone calls will not.

In closing your conversation, take care to ascertain the correct spelling and pronunciation of the interviewer's name. This shows your concern for the small but important things in life—and it will be noticed, particularly when your interviewer receives your follow-up thank-you note. (See the latest edition of *Knock 'em Dead Cover Letters* for a comprehensive selection of sample follow-up letters.)

It is difficult to evaluate an opportunity properly over the phone, so even if the job doesn't sound right, go to the interview; it will give you practice, and the job may look better when you have more facts. You might even discover a more suitable opening elsewhere within the company.

Once you score a face-to-face meeting, there are a lot of preparations to be made. The first of these is preparing your interview wardrobe.

PART TWO

BEFORE THE INTERVIEW

CHAPTER 5

DRESS FOR JOB INTERVIEW SUCCESS

WHEN YOU MAKE THE EFFORT TO DRESS PROFESSIONALLY, there are three results: You look better, you feel better, and others treat you better. That's a good head start to have heading into a job interview.

The moment you set eyes on someone, your mind makes evaluations and judgments with lightning speed. Potential employers also make the same lightning-speed evaluations when you first meet at the beginning of a job interview. It's a fair estimate that nine out of ten of today's employers will reject an unsuitably dressed applicant without a second thought.

"What You See Is What You Get!"

The initial respect you receive at the interview will be in direct proportion to the image you project. The correct professional appearance won't get you the job offer—but it will lend everything you say that much more credence and weight. Wearing a standard business uniform instantly communicates that you understand one of the paramount unwritten rules of professional life, and that you have a confident self-image.

Employers rarely make overt statements about acceptable dress codes to their employees, much less to interviewees. Instead, there is a generally accepted but unspoken dictum that those who wish to succeed will dress appropriately, and those who don't, won't.

There are a few professions where on-the-job dress (as opposed to interview dress) is somewhat less conservative than in the mainstream: Fashion, entertainment, and advertising are three examples. But for 95 percent of us, jobs and employers require a certain level of traditional professionalism in our wardrobes. While you need not dress like the chairman of the board (although that probably wouldn't hurt), adopting "casual Friday" attire on the day of your interview is not in your best professional interests. For a job interview, you should dress one to two levels up from the job you are applying for, while remaining consistent with the type of occupation it is within. To maximize your career options over the long haul of a career, you must aim to consistently meet or exceed these standards.

Your Interview Advantage

Your appearance tells people how you feel about yourself as an applicant, as well as how you feel about the interviewer, the company, and the interview process itself. By dressing professionally, you tell people that you understand the niceties of corporate life, and you send a subtle "reinforcing" message that you can, for example, be relied on to deal one-on-one with members of a company's prized client base.

How you dress sends signals about:

- How seriously you take the occasion, and, by extension, how much respect you have for your interviewers.
- How well you understand the confidence a look of traditional professionalism gives clients, customers, peers, and superiors.

Yet no matter how important these concerns might be, they pale in comparison to the impact a sharp appearance can have on your own sense of self. When you know you have taken care of your appearance and that you look the best you can, you feel pride and confidence: Your posture is better, you smile more, and you feel more "in control" of your destiny. In turn, others will respond positively to the image of professionalism and self-confidence that you present. Portraying the correct image at an interview will give you a real edge over your competition. What you say is reinforced by the way you present yourself. Appearances count.

The Look

The safest look for both men and women at interviews is traditional and conservative. Consider investing in a good-fitting, well-made suit as your first step to a successful strategic career move. With your business clothes, quality matters far more than quantity; it's better to have one good outfit than two mediocre ones. Your professional wardrobe is a long-term career asset, so add quality items, and over time the quantity will come.

Up until recently, this was fairly easy for men, as their professional fashions tended to remain constant. These days, men's fashions are experiencing a metamorphosis, with designers of high fashion offering affordable lines of updated, professionally acceptable looks. However, a man can always interview with confidence and poise in his six-year-old Brooks Brothers suit, provided it isn't worn to a shine.

For women, things are more complicated. Appropriate female attire should reflect current professional fashions if the applicant is to be taken seriously. Moreover, in selecting a current professional look, a woman must walk a fine line, combining elements of both conformity (to show she belongs) and panache (to show a measure of individuality and style).

The key for both sexes is to dress for the position you want, not the one you have. This means the upwardly mobile professional might need to invest in the clothes that project the desired image.

The correct appearance alone probably won't get you a job offer, but it does go a long way toward winning the attention and respect you need to land the offer. When you know you look right, you can stop worrying about the impression your clothes are making and concentrate on communicating your message.

Every interview and interviewer is different, so it isn't possible to set down rigid guidelines for exactly what to wear in any given situation. However, there are a handful of commonsense guidelines that will ensure you are perceived as someone savvy, practical, competent, reliable, and professional.

General Guidelines

The right look varies from industry to industry. A college professor can sport tweed jackets with elbow patches on the job, and an advertising executive may don the latest designer dress or wear wild ties as a badge of creativity (that is what they are being paid for). Nevertheless, that same college professor is likely to wear a suit to an important interview, and even professional men and women in advertising and the media are likely to dress more conservatively for a job interview.

Most of us are far more adept at recognizing the dress mistakes of others than at spotting our own image failings. When you look for a second opinion, you often make the mistake of asking only a loved one. Better candidates for evaluation of your interview attire are trusted professional friends who have proven their objectivity in such matters.

Whenever possible, find out the dress code of the company you are visiting. For example, if you are an engineer applying for a job at a high-tech company, a blue three-piece suit might be overpowering. It is perfectly acceptable to ask someone in Human Resources about the dress code (written or informal) of the company. You may even want to make an anonymous visit to get a sense of the corporate style of the company; if that isn't practical, you can always visit the website to see how the company likes to be perceived by its public.

I have been asked, "If everyone wears sweaters at the company where I am interviewing, shouldn't I wear the same if I want to be seen to fit in?" In fact, very few companies allow a very relaxed dress code for all their employees all the time. An increasing percentage allows a somewhat relaxed dress code on a particular day (often Friday), when "casual professional" attire is allowed, if not always encouraged. Sometimes, some younger professionals mistake this to mean they can dress for the beach at all times. Even if the company is casual all the time for all its employees, do not dress casually for a job interview. There are two big reasons to avoid casual interview attire:

1. The company is considering an investment that will probably run into hundreds of thousands of dollars if the hire works out, and potentially as much as tens of thousands of dollars if it doesn't—hardly a casual event.

2. Companies sometimes allow casual dress at times and in circumstances that will not jeopardize business. They are comfortable doing this because they already know everyone on the payroll knows how to dress appropriately. The interview is where the company needs to know you appreciate the niceties of business dress; they already have a fair idea that you own a sweater and a pair of khakis.

Tattoos and Piercings

If you are contemplating a professional career, recognize that visible body piercings and tattoos will forever close many doors to your entry, and most of the rest to your ascent. While tattoos and piercings are an individual expression and your right, corporations also have a right not to hire people whom they feel are unable to represent company interests in the best light. Like it or not, *any and all body decoration is frowned upon by the vast majority of employers.*

In other words, if you sport tats or piercings, conceal them during the interview and at all times during your professional endeavors. If you are considering body decoration, ask yourself if in the history of humankind there has ever been one item in any man or woman's wardrobe that he or she has willingly worn every day for the rest of his or her life. Soberly weigh your personal interests against your professional success.

Men

The following are the best current dress guidelines for men preparing for a professional interview.

Men's Suits

A *Wall Street Journal* survey of CEOs showed a 53 percent preference for navy blue and dark blue, while 39 percent favored gray or charcoal gray. Brown can be acceptable for subsequent interviews at some companies. In summer months, a lightweight beige suit is fine at second or third interviews; you would never wear a light-colored suit except during the warmer months. Ideally, wear a 100-percent wool suit, as wool looks and wears better than any other material. The darker the suit, the more authority it carries. (Beware: A man should not wear a black suit to an interview unless applying for an undertaker's job.) Pinstripes and solids, in dark gray, navy, or medium blue, are equally acceptable, although many feel a dark solid suit is the best option because it gives authority to the wearer and is seen as less stuffy than a pinstripe suit. Somewhat less common but also acceptable are gray-colored glen plaid (also called "Prince of Wales") or hound's-tooth suits.

A two-piece suit is the safest choice. Double-breasted jackets are seen as more edgy, and you are more likely to wear them to an interview at an advertising agency than at the local bank. Above all, it's the quality and fit of your suit that matters. Current fashions favor a slimmer cut, particularly in the trousers. However, the fit and cut must complement your build. The leaner, tapered look elongates your appearance; the looser cuts add bulk. There should be no pull at the jacket shoulders and no gape at the back, and the jacket cuffs should break at your wrists. Your trousers should fit comfortably at the waist. A flat front is most flattering (unless you are enviably scrawny), and there should be only a slight break where the trouser hits the shoe. If your ankles are visible in the mirror, the pants are too damn short! Cuffed trousers add a very sophisticated and conservative look, but an important consideration might be that un-cuffed trousers add height.

Men's Shirts

The principles here are simple:

- **Rule One:** Always wear a long-sleeved shirt; never wear a short-sleeved shirt.
- **Rule Two:** Always wear a white, cream, or pale blue shirt.

By white, I do not mean to exclude, for instance, shirts with very thin red or blue pinstripes; nevertheless, there is a presence about a solid white shirt that seems to convey honesty, intelligence, and stability; it should be your first choice. It is true that artists, writers, software engineers, and other creative types are sometimes known to object to white shirts because they feel that it makes it look like "the suit is wearing them." If this is you and you can't get over it, pale blue may be the best option. Remember—the paler and more subtle the shade, the better the impression you will make. Pale colors draw attention, and your collar is right next to your face, which is where you want the interviewer to stay focused.

While monograms are common enough, those who don't wear them may feel strongly about the implied ostentation of stylized initials on clothing; the great valet Jeeves once commented on the topic, saying, "I thought the practice was restricted to those in danger of forgetting their names."

Cotton shirts look better and hold up under perspiration more impressively than their synthetic counterparts. If at all possible, opt for a cotton shirt that has been professionally cleaned and starched. A cotton and polyester blend can be an acceptable alternative, but keep in mind that the higher the cotton content, the better the shirt will look. While blend shirts wrinkle less easily, you are advised to ignore the "wash-and-wear" and "no need to iron" claims you'll read on the front of the package when you purchase them.

Make sure your shirt fits the neck properly; the sleeve cuff should end at the wrist. Details such as frayed fabric and loose buttons will not go unnoticed when you are under professional scrutiny. It's best to choose your interview clothes well in advance, make any minor repairs, have them cleaned, and keep them ready.

Ties

Just as a cheap-looking tie can ruin an expensive suit, the right tie can do a lot to pull the less-than-perfect suit together for a professional look. When you can't afford a new suit for the interview, you can upgrade your whole look with the right tie.

A pure silk tie makes the most powerful professional impact, has the best finish and feel, and is easiest to tie well. A pure silk tie or a 50 percent wool/50 percent silk blend (which is almost wrinkle-proof) should be your choice for the interview. Linen ties are too informal, can only be tied once or twice between cleanings because they wrinkle easily, and only look right during warmer weather anyway. A wool tie is casual in appearance and has knot problems. Most man-made fibers are too shiny, with harsh colors that may undercut your professional image.

The tie should complement your suit. This means that there should be a physical balance: The rule of thumb is that the width of your tie should approximate the width of your lapels. The prevailing standard, which has held for over a decade now, is that ties can range in width between 2½ and 3½ inches. Wearing anything wider may mark you as someone still trapped in the disco era. Currently, ties are being worn narrower in the pages of the fashion magazines, but that really doesn't have to concern you.

While the tie should complement the suit, it should not match it. You would never, for instance, wear a navy blue tie with a navy blue suit. Choose an appropriate tie that neither vanishes into nor battles with your suit pattern or color. The most popular and safest styles are solids, very small prints (foulards), stripes, and paisleys.

Do not wear ties with large polka dots, pictures of animals such as leaping trout or soaring mallards, or sporting symbols such as golf clubs or (God forbid) little men on polo ponies. Avoid wearing any piece of apparel that has a manufacturer's symbol emblazoned on the front as part of the decoration.

Other considerations include the length of the tie (it should, when tied, extend to your trouser belt), the size of the knot (smaller is better), and whether you should wear a bow tie to an interview (you shouldn't).

Men's Shoes

Shoes should be either black leather or brown leather. Stay away from all other materials and colors. Lace-up wingtips are the most universally acceptable. Slightly less conservative, but equally appropriate, are slip-on dress shoes—not to be confused with boating shoes. The slip-on, with its low, plain vamp or tassel is versatile enough to be used for both day and evening business wear. Those who are hyperconscious of fashion will say that a lace-up wingtip can look a bit cloddish at dinner. This may be true if you have a dinner interview with the senior partner of a law firm in Chicago, Los Angeles, or New York, but otherwise, don't lose sleep over it.

In certain areas of the South, Southwest, and West, heeled cowboy boots are not at all unusual for business wear, and neither are those Grand Ole Opry versions of the business suit. But beware: Outside of Dallas, Nashville, Muskogee, and similar municipalities, you will attract only puzzled stares—so try to be aware of the regional variations in professional dress.

Men's Socks

Socks should complement the suit. Accordingly, they should be blue, black, gray, or brown. When they match the suit color, they extend the length of your leg, giving more height and authority. They should also be long enough for you to cross your legs without showing off bare skin, and should not fall in a bunch toward the ankle as you move. Elastic-reinforced, over-the-calf socks are your best bet.

Men's Accessories

The right accessories can enhance the professional image of any applicant, male or female, just as the wrong accessories can destroy it. The guiding principle here is to include nothing that could be misconstrued or leave a bad impression. For instance, you should not wear obvious religious or political insignias in the form of rings, ties, or pins, as they draw attention to matters that employers are forbidden to address by federal law. This does not necessarily apply when you are aware that a particular spiritual association will establish connectivity, such as wearing a cross when you interview with the Archdiocese.

The watch you wear should be simple and preferably plain, which means that funky Mickey Mouse is out. Sports watches or digital monsters are acceptable nowadays but aren't the best choice. Don't be afraid to wear a simple, slim watch with a leather strap; you will notice it is what the most successful and sophisticated business professionals wear.

A briefcase is always perceived as a symbol of authority and can make a strong professional statement. Leather makes the best impression, with brown and burgundy being the colors of choice. The case is best unadorned—embellishments can only detract from the effect of quiet confidence and authority.

It's a good idea to take a cotton or linen handkerchief on all interviews. Plain white is best because it looks crisp, but the color isn't really that important. You aren't taking a handkerchief to put in a breast pocket, but for far more practical reasons. That handkerchief can be used to relieve the clammy-hands syndrome so common before an interview—anything to avoid the infamous "wet fish" handshake. Keep it in an inside pocket, avoiding the matching tie-and-pocket-square look of a dyed-in-the-wool doofus at all costs.

Belts should match or complement the shoes you select. Accordingly, a blue or gray suit will require a black belt and black shoes, while brown, tan, or beige suits call for brown. Wear a good-quality leather belt if you can. The most common mistake made with belts is the buckle; an interview is not the place for your favorite Harley Davidson, Grateful Dead, or Bart Simpson buckle. Select a small, simple buckle that doesn't overwhelm the rest of your look or make personal statements that you cannot be certain will resonate with an interviewer.

Men's Jewelry

Men may wear a wedding band, and cuff links are acceptable with French cuffs. Anything more in the way of jewelry can be dangerous. Necklaces, bracelets, neck chains, and earrings can send the wrong message, and tie tacks and clips are passé in most areas of the country.

Men's Raincoats

The safest and most utilitarian colors for raincoats are beige and blue; stick to these two exclusively. If you can avoid wearing a raincoat, do so (it's an encumbrance and adds to clutter), but it is better to have a raincoat than to have your suit drenched.

Women

Following are the best current dress guidelines for women preparing for a professional interview.

Women's Suits

You have more room for creativity in this area than men do, but also more room for mistakes. Until recent years, professional fashion creativity had to remain within certain accepted guidelines dictated not by the fashion industry, but by the consensus of the business world— which trails far behind the pages of fashion magazines. And while there are still the limits of good taste and necessary conservatism for the interviewer, fashion designers have worked hard to create workable professional alternatives for the ever-growing female workforce.

A woman's business wardrobe need no longer be simply a pseudo-male selection of drab gray skirts and blouses. With the right cuts, pinstripes and menswear-inspired fashions can look both stylish and professional.

Wool and linen are both accepted as the right look for professional women's suits, but linen can present a problem. Linen wrinkles so quickly that you may feel as though you leave the house dressed for success and arrive at your destination looking like a bag lady. Cotton-polyester blends are great for warm climates; they look like linen but lack the wrinkle factor. Combinations of synthetics and natural fabrics have their advantages: Suits made of such material will certainly retain their shape better. The eye trained to pay attention to detail, however (read: the interviewer's), may detect the type of fabric—say, a cheap polyester blend—and draw unwarranted conclusions about your personality and taste. The choice is up to you. If you do opt for natural fabrics, you will probably want to stay with wool. It provides the smartest look of all and is most versatile and rugged. There are wonderful, ultra-light wool gabardines available now that will take you through the toughest interview on the hottest summer day.

Like her male counterpart, the professional woman should stick to solids or pinstripes in gray, navy, and medium blues. The ubiquitous Prince of Wales plaid (glen plaid) or hound's-tooth check can both look very distinguished on a woman as well. At the same time, a much wider palette of colors is open for consideration by the professional woman. While there are situations where you will want to choose one of the more powerful colors, it might be best at one of the subsequent interviews, rather than the first.

A solid skirt with a coordinating subtle plaid jacket is also acceptable, but make sure there is not too much contrast or it will detract from the focus of your meeting: the interview. Colors most suitable for interview suits include charcoal, medium gray, steel gray, black (whereas a man is advised against black, the color is open and acceptable for the professional woman), and navy blue. Of all these looks, the cleanest and most professional is the simple solid navy or gray suit with a white blouse.

Jackets should be simple, well tailored, and stylish, but not stylized. This is probably not the time to wear a peplum-style jacket—a standard length that falls just at the hips is preferable. The cut and style should flatter your build and reflect your personal style without detracting from what you have to say. Attention to details such as smooth seams, even hemlines, correctly hanging linings, and well-sewn buttons are essential.

How long a skirt should you wear? Any hard-and-fast rule I could offer here would be outdated almost immediately, as the fashion industry demands dramatically different looks every season in order to fuel sales. It should go without saying that you don't want to sport something that soars to the upper thigh if you want to be taken seriously as an applicant. Your best bet is to dress somewhat more conservatively than you would if you were simply showing up for work at the organization in question. Hemlines come and go, and while there is some leeway as to what is appropriate for everyday wear on the job, the safest bet is usually to select something that falls at or no more than two inches above the knee.

Increasingly popular is the dress with a matching jacket. This outfit is particularly useful for the "business day into evening" crowd, but can be perfectly suitable for interviews if it is properly styled and fitted. It is particularly important to stick with subtle solid colors for this look.

Dress Shirts

Dress shirts with long sleeves will project a responsible and professional look. Three-quarter-length sleeves are less desirable, followed in turn by short sleeves. Never wear a sleeveless blouse to an interview; you may be confident that there is absolutely no chance that you will be required to remove your jacket, but why take the risk of offending someone with unexpected glimpses of undergarments?

Solid colors and natural fabrics, particularly cotton and silk, are the best selections for blouses—although silk is warm and therefore raises perspiration concerns for a nervous interviewee. Combinations of natural and synthetic fabrics are wrinkle-resistant but do not absorb moisture well, so with these choices you will need to take perspiration countermeasures into account.

The acceptable color spectrum is wider for women's shirts than for men's, but it is not limitless. The most prudent choices are still white or cream or gray; these offer a universal professional appeal. Pale pink or light blue can also work, but should be worn only if it fully blends into your overall look. Light colors are "friendly" and draw attention to your face, yet will not distract the interviewer from what you have to say. A classic softened shirt collar works best with a suit. Also, the button-down collar always looks great, particularly if you are interviewing with a conservative company or industry.

Women's Neckwear

While a woman might choose to wear a string of pearls instead of a scarf to an interview, the scarf can still serve as a powerful status symbol. Opting to wear a scarf says something dramatic about you; make sure it's something positive. A pure silk scarf will offer a conservative look, a good finish, and ease in tying. Some of the better synthetic blends achieve an overall effect that is almost as good. Avoid overly flamboyant styles, and stick with solids or basic prints (very small prints [foulards], small polka dots, or paisleys) in subtle colors that will complement—not compete with—your outfit or your conversation.

Women's Shoes

The professional woman has a greater color selection in footwear than does her male counterpart. The shoes should preferably be leather, but in addition to brown and black, a woman is safe in wearing navy, gray, or burgundy. Good-quality black patent leather is acceptable for winter.

It is safest to stay away from faddish or multicolored shoes (even such classics as two-toned oxfords). First, all fashion is transitory, and even if you are up-to-date, you cannot assume that your interviewer is. Second, a good proportion of your interviewers might be men, who are less likely to appreciate vivid color combinations. As with the rest of your wardrobe, stay away from radical choices and opt for the easily comprehensible professional look.

Heel height is important as well. Flats are fine; a shoe with a heel of up to about 2½ inches is perfectly acceptable. Stay away from higher heels; at best you will wobble slightly, and at worst you will walk at an angle. The pump, with its closed toe and heel, is perhaps the safest and most conservative look. A conservative peep-toe pump is acceptable, too, as is the slingback shoe with a closed toe. The toe on any style should not be overly pointed. Just think moderation in all things; the goal is to get hired, not dated.

Pantyhose

These should not make their own statement. Neutral skin tones are the safest, most conservative choice, though you are perfectly within the realm of professional etiquette to wear off-black if it complements your shirt or dress. You may make an exception if you are interviewing for a job in the fashion industry, in which case you might coordinate colors with your outfit, but be very sure of the company dress code that is already in place. Even in such an instance, avoid loud or glitzy looks.

As you well know, pantyhose and stockings are prone to developing runs at the worst possible moment, so keep an extra pair in your purse or briefcase.

Women's Accessories

Because a briefcase is a symbol of authority, it is an excellent choice for the professional woman. Do not, however, bring both your purse and a briefcase to the interview (you'll look awkward juggling them). Instead, transfer essential items to a small clutch bag you can store in the case. In addition to brown and burgundy (recommended colors for the men), you may include black and navy as possible colors for your case, which should always be free of personal, expensive, or distracting embellishments.

Belts should match or complement the shoes you select. A black or gray suit will require a black belt and black shoes; brown, tan, or beige suits will call for brown; and navy looks best with navy or burgundy accessories. In addition, women may wear snakeskin, lizard, and the like (though beware of offending animal rights activists). Remember that the belt is a functional item; if it is instantly noticeable, it is wrong.

Women's Jewelry

Less is more. A woman should restrict rings to engagement or wedding bands if these are applicable. All other jewelry should be subdued, professional-looking, and in good taste. Avoid oversized pieces, fashion jewelry, dangle earrings, initialed jewelry, and anything that makes noise. You should also remove any kind of visible body piercing except for earrings in the earlobe. Remember, too much of the wrong kind of jewelry could cost you a job offer or inhibit your promotional opportunities once on the team.

Makeup

Take care never to appear overly made-up; "natural" is the key word. Eye makeup should be subtle, so as not to overwhelm the rest of the face. As a general rule, I advise very little lipstick at an interview because it can cause negative reactions in some interviewers, and because it can smudge and wear off as the hours wear on. (Who can say, going in, how long the meeting will last?) However, women tell me that as they advance into their thirties and beyond, the natural pinkness of the lips can fade; you might feel you look pale and washed-out without lipstick. So if you feel "undressed" without your lipstick, use some: But apply it sparingly and carefully, choose a neutral or subdued color, and, of course, never apply it in public.

If you have a tattoo in a conspicuous place, it could be offensive to an interviewer and it could cause you not to be taken seriously. You should dress to cover your ink, and if that is not possible, invest in a make-up product specially designed for hiding tattoos such as Derma-Blend.

For Men and Women: A Note on Personal Hygiene

Bad breath, dandruff, body odor, and dirty, unmanicured nails have the potential to undo all your efforts at giving a good first impression. These and related problems all speak to an underlying slovenliness, which an interviewer may feel will manifest itself in your work. You want to present yourself as an appealing, self-respecting, and enjoyable professional to be around. You can't achieve this if the people you meet have to call on their powers of self-control in order to stay in the same room with you.

What was that old TV body odor commercial tagline? "What even your best friend won't tell you." So don't ask yourself whether any friend or colleague has actually come out and suggested that you pay more attention to personal hygiene; it is such a touchy issue that most people will avoid you rather than discuss it. Ask yourself how you felt the last time you had to conduct business of any sort with someone who had a hygiene problem. Then resolve never to leave that kind of impression.

Personal grooming of hair, skin, teeth, and nails is easy and straightforward, but body odor is a different challenge. When it comes to body odor, you are literally what you eat—thus, onions, garlic, junk food, alcohol, and coffee can all give your bodily odors a distinctly unpleasant pungency. Because it takes time for your body to rid itself of such smells, the best advice is to start paying attention to diet as you begin to put your wardrobe together.

If you are a smoker, do take into consideration that a non-smoking interviewer, especially in a company that declares itself a "smoke-free workplace," may be offended by cigarette odor. Be mindful of lingering smoke smells that cling to your person and to your clothing. Avoid smoking in a contained area before an interview, have your interview attire professionally cleaned, do not smoke while wearing it, and do not store it in an area of your home in which anyone smokes.

Now that you know how to dress professionally, it's time to look at another essential communication skill: body language. Learning how it can work against you and how to make it work for you is vital for turning interviews into job offers.

CHAPTER 6

BODY LANGUAGE

WHILE SPEECH IS A COMPARATIVELY RECENT DEVELOPMENT, humans have been sending and receiving nonverbal signals since the dawn of our species, and the language of our bodies is the first means of communication we develop. We gain mastery of body language so early that it becomes a subconscious skill.

Verbal communication dominates in the professional world—but nonverbal signals are still sent and received, and we all still interpret and respond to them, some more than others, and skilled interviewers more than most.

If you are job hunting (or mate hunting, for that matter), you should recognize that your body is constantly sending messages, and make every effort to understand and control the information stream. If your mouth says, "Hire me," but your body says, "I'm not being truthful," you are likely to leave the interviewer confused. "Well," she will think, "the right answers all came out, but there was something about that candidate that just rubbed me the wrong way." Such misgivings are generally sufficient to keep a candidate from getting the job offer. The evaluation might not even be expressed negatively; the hiring manager might just prefer another candidate, in part because of that candidate's positive body language.

Of course, interviewers will listen carefully to what you say, too. When your body language complements your verbal statements, your message will gain a great deal of impact, but when your body language *contradicts* what you say, the interviewer will be skeptical. In short, learning to use positive body signals and control negative ones during an interview can have a significant impact on your ability to turn job interviews into job offers.

Your Body Makes Powerful First Impressions

The challenge for the interviewer is to determine, using every means at his disposal, what kind of an employee you would make. Your task as a candidate is to provide the clues most likely to prompt a decision to hire.

Let's begin at the beginning. When you are invited to an interview, you are probably safe in assuming that your interviewer believes you meet certain minimum standards and could conceivably be hired.

In this context, the adage that actions speak louder than words should be taken quite literally. Studies done at the University of Chicago found that over 50 percent of all effective communication relies on body language. Since you can expect interviewers to respond to the body language you employ at the interview, it is up to you to decide what messages you want them to receive.

There are also studies that suggest the impression you create in the first few minutes of the interview is the most lasting. Since the first few minutes after you meet the interviewer is a time when she is doing the vast majority of the talking, you have very little control over the impression you create with your words—you can't say much of anything! It is up to your body to do the job for you.

The Greeting
For a good handshake:

1. Your hands should be clean and your nails trimmed.
2. Your hands should be dry.

Certain professional differences should also be considered in greeting: Many doctors, dentists, artists, and others who do delicate work with their hands can and do give less enthusiastic handshakes than other people. If you work in the media, you'll notice that many on-air personalities don't want to shake hands at all: It's the easiest way to catch a cold, and they depend on their voices and appearance more than most.

It is normal for the host (interviewer) to initiate the handshake, smile confidently, and make eye contact. Match the pressure extended by the interviewer—never exceed it. A typical professional handshake lasts between two and five seconds, just two or three reasonably firm up-and-down pumps accompanied by a smile. Your handshake should signal cooperation and friendliness.

Use only one hand and always shake vertically. Do not extend your hand parallel to the floor with the palm up, as this conveys submissiveness. By the same token, you may be seen as too aggressive if you extend your hand outward with the palm facing down.

While a confident and positive handshake helps break the ice and gets the interview moving in the right direction, proper use of the hands throughout the rest of the interview will help convey an above-board, "nothing-to-hide" message.

Employing your hands in these positive ways can further your candidacy:

- Subtly exposing your palms now and then as you speak can help demonstrate that you are open, friendly, and have nothing to hide. You can see this technique used to great effect by politicians and television talk show hosts.
- It can, very occasionally, be beneficial to "steeple" your fingers for a few seconds as you consider a question or when you first start to talk. Unless you hold the gesture for long periods of time, it will be perceived as a neutral demonstration of your thoughtfulness. Of course, if you overuse or hold this position for too long, you may be taken as condescending. Steepling also gives you something

constructive to do with your hands; it offers a change from holding your pad and pen.

Negative hand messages include:

- Hands and fingers that take on a life of their own, fidgeting with themselves or other objects such as pens, paper, or your hair. Pen tapping is interpreted as the action of an impatient person—this is a good example of an otherwise trivial habit that can take on immense significance in an interview situation. Rarely will an interviewer ask you to stop doing something annoying. Instead, he'll simply make a mental note that you are an annoying person and congratulate himself for picking up on this before making the mistake of hiring you.
- Clasping your hands behind your head. You'll expose perspiration marks, and you run the risk of appearing smug, superior, bored, and possibly withdrawn.
- Showing insecurity by constantly adjusting your tie. When interviewing with a woman, this gesture could be interpreted as displaying something beyond a businesslike interest in the interviewer.
- Slouching in your chair, with hands in pockets or thumbs in belt. This posture can brand you as insolent and aggressive (think of any teenage boy). When this error is made in the presence of an interviewer of the opposite sex, it can carry sexually aggressive overtones as well.
- Pulling your collar away from your neck. This may seem like an innocent enough reaction on a hot day, but the way we interpret body language signals may lead the interviewer to assume that you are tense or masking an untruth. The same goes for scratching your neck during, before, or after your response to a question.
- Moving your hands toward a personal feature that you perceive as deficient. This is a common unconscious reaction to stress. A man with thinning hair, for example, may thoughtlessly put his hand to his forehead when pondering how to respond to a query ("Why aren't you earning more at your age?"). This habit may be extremely difficult for

you to detect in the first place, much less reverse, but make the effort. Such protective movements are likely to be perceived—if only on a subliminal level—as an acknowledgment of low self-esteem.

- Picking at invisible bits of fluff on your clothing or otherwise rearranging your immediate environment. This is a nervous tic that friends and family have gotten used to, but others find a little weird. If you have a touch of OCD, get a friend to help you identify these kinds of repetitive gestures that interviewers might find annoying.

Taking Your Seat

Some thirty inches from my nose

The frontier of my person goes.

Beware of rudely crossing it,

I have no gun, but I can spit.

—W. H. Auden

Encroaching on another's "personal space" is a bad idea in any business situation, but it is particularly dangerous in an interview. The thirty-inch standard is a good one to follow: It is the distance that allows you to extend your hand comfortably for a handshake. Maintain this distance throughout the interview, and be particularly watchful of personal-space intrusions when you first meet, greet, and take a seat.

A person's office is an extension of his personal zone; this is why it is not only polite but also sound business sense to wait until the interviewer offers you a seat.

It is not uncommon to meet with an interviewer in a conference room or another supposedly "neutral" site. Again, wait for the interviewer to motion you to a spot, or, if you feel uncomfortable doing this, tactfully ask the interviewer to take the initiative: "Where would you like me to sit?"

The type of chair you sit in can affect the signals your body sends during an interview. If you have a choice, go with an upright chair with arms. Deep armchairs can restrict your ability to send certain positive signals and encourage the likelihood of slumping. They're best suited for watching television, not for projecting the image of a competent professional.

Always sit with your bottom well back in the chair and your back straight. Slouching, as we have noted, is out, but a slight forward-leaning posture will show interest and friendliness toward the interviewer. Keep your hands quietly employed, perhaps resting on the arms of the chair; if there are no arms on the chair, keep your hands in your lap or occupied with paper and pen. This latter not only gives you something to do with your hands, it makes you look organized and gives you the ability to jot down notes or questions.

Crossed Legs

Crossed legs, in all their many forms, send a mixture of signals; most of them are negative:

- Crossing one ankle over the other knee can show a certain stubborn and recalcitrant outlook (as well as the bottom of your shoe, which is not always a pretty sight). The negative signal is intensified when you grasp the horizontally crossed leg or—worst of all—cross your arms across your chest.
- Some body language experts feel crossed ankles indicate that the person doing the crossing is withholding information. Of course, since the majority of interviews take place across a desk, crossed ankles will often be virtually unnoticeable. For women, some dress fashions encourage decorous ankle crossing. This posture is probably the most permissible body language faux pas, so if you must allow yourself one body language vice, this is the one to choose.
- When sitting in armchairs or on sofas, crossing the legs may be necessary to create some stability amid all the plush upholstery. In this instance, the signals you send by crossing your legs will be neutral, as long as your legs are not crossed ankle over knee.

Facial Signals

Once you and the interviewer take your seats and the conversation begins, the interviewer's attention will be focused on your face.

Our language is full of expressions testifying to the powerful influence of facial mannerisms. When you say that someone is shifty-eyed, tight-lipped, has a furrowed brow, flashes bedroom eyes, stares into space, or grins like an idiot, you are speaking in a kind of shorthand and using a set of archetypes that enable you to make judgments—consciously or unconsciously—about that person.

Tight smiles and tension in the facial muscles often bespeak an inability to handle stress; little eye contact can communicate personal insecurity or desire to hide something; pursed lips are often associated with a secretive nature; while frowning, looking sideways, or peering over one's glasses can send signals of haughtiness and arrogance. Hardly the stuff of which winning interviews are made!

Eye Signals

Looking at someone means showing interest in that person, and showing interest is a giant step forward in making the right impression. Remember: We are all our own favorite subjects!

Looking away from the interviewer for long periods while she is talking, closing your eyes while being addressed, and repeatedly shifting your focus from the interviewer to some other point are all likely to leave the wrong impression.

There is a difference between looking and staring at someone. Rather than looking at the speaker straight on at all times, create a mental triangle incorporating both of the eyes and the mouth; your eyes will follow a natural, continuous path along the three points. Maintain this approach for roughly three-quarters of the time; you can break your gaze to look at the interviewer's hands as points are emphasized or to refer to your notepad. This is the way we maintain eye contact in nonstressful situations, and it will allow you to appear attentive, sincere, and committed.

Be wary of breaking eye contact too abruptly and of shifting your focus in ways that will disrupt the atmosphere of professionalism.

Examining the interviewer below the head and shoulders, for instance, is a sign of overfamiliarity. This is especially important to remember when being interviewed by someone of the opposite sex.

Head Movements

Nodding your head slowly shows interest, validates your interviewer's comments, and subtly encourages him to continue. Tilting the head slightly, when combined with eye contact and a natural smile, demonstrates friendliness and approachability. The tilt should be momentary and not exaggerated, almost like a bob of the head to one side. (Do not overuse this technique unless you are applying for a job in a parrot shop.) Rapidly nodding your head can leave the impression that you are impatient and eager to add something to the conversation if only the interviewer would let you; if an interviewer does this, you need to wrap up your point and return control of the conversation to her.

Mouth Signals

The guiding principle of good body language is to turn your mouth upward rather than downward. Look at two boxers after a fight: The victor's arms are raised high, his back is straight, and his shoulders are square. His smiling face is thrust upward and outward, and you see happiness, openness, warmth, and confidence. The loser, on the other hand, is slumped forward, brows knit and eyes downcast, and the signals you receive are those of anger, frustration, belligerence, and defeat.

Your smile is one of the most powerful positive body signals in your arsenal, and it exemplifies the up-is-best principle. Offer an unforced, confident smile as frequently as opportunity and circumstance allow, but avoid grinning idiotically, as this indicates that you may not be quite right in the head.

You should be aware that the mouth also provides a seemingly limitless supply of opportunities to convey weakness. Touching the mouth frequently, "faking" a cough when confronted with a difficult question, or gnawing on one's lips absentmindedly may do this.

Employing any of these "insincerity signs" when you are asked about, say, why you lost your last job, might instill or confirm suspicions about your honesty or openness.

Glasses

People who wear glasses sometimes leave them off when going on an interview in an attempt to project a more favorable image. There are difficulties with this approach. Farsighted people who don't wear their glasses will (unwittingly) seem to stare long and hard at the people they converse with, and this is a negative signal. Also, pulling out glasses for reading and peering over the top of your glasses—even if you have been handed something to read and subsequently asked a question—carries professorial connotations that can be interpreted as critical. If you wear glasses for reading, you should remove them when conversing, replacing them only when appropriate.

Wearing dark glasses to an interview will paint you as secretive, cold, and devious. Even if your prescription glasses are tinted, the effect will be the same. You might consider untinted glasses for your interview, or contacts. At the same time, glasses on a younger-looking person can add an air of seriousness and might be considered a plus.

Body Barricade Signals

Folding or crossing your arms, or holding things in front of your body, sends negative messages to the interviewer: "I know you're there, but you can't come in. I'm nervous and closed for business."

It is bad enough to feel this way, but worse to express it with blatant signals. Don't fold your arms or "protect" your chest with hands, briefcase, or anything else during the interview. You can, however, keep a pad and pen on your lap, since it makes you look organized and gives you something to do with your hands.

Foot Signals

Your feet should intrude on the interview as little as possible. There is little they can do that is overtly positive in a professional environment and there are a couple of foot signals that can send negative messages.

Women and men wearing slip-on shoes should beware of dangling the loose shoe from the toes; this can be distracting, and, as it is a gesture often used to signal physical attraction, it has no place in a job interview.

Likewise, avoid compulsive jabbing of floor, desk, or chair with your foot; this can be perceived as a hostile and angry motion, and is likely to annoy the interviewer.

Some of us (and I'm one of "us") have something called nervous leg syndrome. Sit me at a desk and one leg will be flexed at the knee snapping up and down like the drummer in a thrash metal band shredding the hell out of that bass drum. I'm ADHD with a touch of OCD thrown in and this is typical of many of my fellow travelers. Now, if you are one of us, you know it is nothing more than a soothing soundtrack to the beat of an agile mind, but to others it can be annoying and offensive. It is something you need to consciously control at job interviews, or it will cost you job offers.

The solution is to give a friend/loved one permission to call you on it every time you start drumming. Learn to be conscious of when you are doing it, and don't do it at any point during a job interview. It is an indulgence that you can overcome . . . at least when you have to deal with the rhythmless at job interviews ;-)

Signals You Send When Walking or Standing

Many interviews will require that you walk from one place to another—on a guided tour of facilities, from one office to another, or to and from the table in a restaurant. How long these walks last is not as important as how you use them to reinforce positive professional behaviors and impressions.

Posture is your main concern: Keep your shoulders back and stay erect. Smile and make eye contact as appropriate.

Walks often include pauses to talk or look at some point of interest. Avoid fidgeting with your feet, rubbing one shoe against the other, or kicking absentmindedly at random objects or the ground; these signals will be distracting to your interviewer and may lead to a belief that you are anxious or insecure.

Crossing your arms or legs while standing carries the same negative connotations as it does when you are sitting. Hands-in-pockets, hands-on-hips, or thumbs-in-belt postures send messages that you are aggressive and trying to dominate. No interviewer wants to hire such a potential management and team-disruption problem.

Putting It All Together

Let's reduce all this information into a handful of simple recommendations. Positive signals reinforce one another; employing them in combination yields an overwhelmingly positive message that is truly greater than the sum of its parts.

So far, we have focused primarily on the pitfalls to avoid—but what messages *should* you send, and how? Here are seven general suggestions on good body language for the interview:

1. Walk slowly and stand tall upon entering the room.
2. On greeting your interviewer, give a smile, make eye contact, and respond warmly to the interviewer's greeting and handshake.
3. As you sit, get your butt well back in the chair; this allows the chair back to help you sit upright. Increase the impression of openness ("I have nothing to hide!") by unbuttoning your jacket as you sit down. Keep your head up. Maintain eye contact a good portion of the time, especially when the interviewer begins to speak and when you reply. Smile naturally whenever the opportunity arises.
4. Use mirroring techniques to reproduce the positive signals your interviewer sends. Say the interviewer leans forward to make a point; a few moments later, you, too, lean forward slightly, demonstrating that you don't want to miss a word. Perhaps the interviewer leans back and laughs; you "laugh beneath" the interviewer's laughter, taking care not to overwhelm your partner by using an inappropriate volume level. This can seem

contrived at first, but through observing those in your own social circle, you'll notice that this is natural behavior for good communicators.

5. Keep your head up and don't slouch in your seat.
6. Try to remain calm and do not hurry your movements; you'll look harried and are more likely to knock things over. Most people are klutzy when they are nervous, and consciously slowing your body movements will lessen the chances of disaster and give you a more controlled persona.
7. Remember to breathe. When we are nervous, we can forget to do this, which leads to oxygen deprivation and obviously screws up cognitive processes.

Open for Business

The more open your body movements during the interview, the more you will be perceived as open yourself. Understanding and directing your body language will give you added power to turn interviews into cooperative exchanges between two professionals.

Just as you interpret the body language of others, both positive and negative, your body language makes an indelible impression on those you meet. It tells them whether you like and have confidence in yourself, whether you are pleasant to be around, and whether you are more likely to be honest or deceitful. Like it or not, your body carries these messages for the world to see.

Parting

A typical professional handshake lasts for between two and five seconds, just two or three reasonably firm up-and-down pumps accompanied by a smile. The parting handshake may last a little longer; smile and lean forward *very* slightly as you shake hands before departing.

Job interviews are reliable in one way: They bring out insecurities. All the more reason to consciously manage the impressions your body sends. You will absorb the lessons in this chapter very quickly if you take the time to observe and interpret the body signals of friends and family. When you see and can understand body language in others, you'll be more aware of your own, and more capable of controlling it.

Once you've internalized the important lessons of the previous two chapters on your physical appearance and conduct, you're almost ready to head to the interview. In the next chapter, we will put together an interview kit, make some final preparations, and get psyched to go turn that interview into a job offer.

CHAPTER 7

THE CURTAIN RISES
ON THE JOB INTERVIEW

BACKSTAGE IN THE THEATER, the announcement "Places, please" is made five minutes before the curtain rises. It's the performers' signal to psych themselves up, complete final costume adjustments, and make time to reach the stage. They are getting ready to go onstage and *knock 'em dead*. You should go through a similar process to get thoroughly prepared for your time in the spotlight, only you should begin two or three days in advance of the interview.

Interview nerves are to be expected; the trick is to harness this nervous energy, like performers do before a performance, to your physical and mental preparation. As the interview approaches, settle down with your resume and TJD exercises. A review of your TJD will remind you:

- What is important to interviewers
- The areas they are likely to question
- How you execute your job to prevent problems from occurring
- Examples of your achievements and the problems you dealt with to accomplish them
- The behavioral profile of the person everyone wants to work with
- The behavioral profile that spells career failure

Sit with your resume and immerse yourself in these considerations and the professional experiences that will support your candidacy, identifying the *transferable skills* and *professional values* that underlie your professional competency in each area.

Check Your Appearance

Your dress should be clean-cut and conservative, as we discussed in Chapter 5. Keep your interview outfit freshly cleaned, shirts or blouses wrinkle-free, shoes polished, and all readied for an interview at a moment's notice. And always double-check them at least one day in advance of the interview.

Visit the hairdresser every month so that you always look groomed, and keep your nails clean and trimmed at all times (even if you work with your hands). While you will naturally shower or bathe prior to an interview, and the use of an unscented deodorant is advisable, you should avoid wearing aftershave or perfume; you are trying to get a job, not a date. Never drink alcohol the day before an interview; it affects your wits and appearance, especially eyes and skin tone.

What to Take

- *The company dossier*: Print out any information you have about the company and its operations, since you are likely to be asked what you know about the company. Visit the company website, review any company literature and research you might have, and do Google and Google Media searches for news articles mentioning the company by name, as well as for articles that relate to your profession.
- *Your resume*: Always take copies of the resume you customized for this job, and perhaps an executive briefing that clearly defines how you match the job's requirements: one for you and one for each of the interviewers you might meet (see *Knock 'em Dead Resumes*).

Your main interviewer will invariably have a copy of your resume, but you can't be certain of that with other people you meet. It is perfectly acceptable to have your resume in front of you at the interview; it shows you are organized, and it makes a great reference sheet when the interviewer refers to your resume.

- *A decent folder with pad of paper and writing instruments*: These demonstrate your preparedness, and they give you something constructive to do with your hands during the interview. You can keep your resume in the folder.
- *Reference letters*: If you have reference letters from past employers, take them along. Some employers don't put much stock in written references and prefer a one-on-one conversation with past employers. Nevertheless, having them with you and getting them placed in your candidate file can't do any harm.
- *A list of job-related questions*: Asking questions that give you insight into the day-to-day challenges of the job shows your engagement with the work. It also helps you advance your candidacy, because judgments about you will be based, in part, on the questions you ask, since your questions demonstrate the depth of your interest and understanding of the job. Additionally, asking questions gives you insight into how you should best focus your answers to the interviewer's queries. You can find a list of appropriate questions in Chapter 14. (*Note*: In the early rounds of interviewing, stay away from questions about where the job can lead and what the pay and benefits are. It's not that these questions aren't important, just that the timing is wrong. It won't do you any good to know what a job pays if you fail to get a job offer. Instead, ask the questions that will help you move toward a job offer being extended, and *then* ask the questions you need to evaluate that offer; you'll find questions to ask during negotiation in that chapter, toward the end of the book.)
- *Directions to the interview*: Decide on your form of transportation and finalize your time of departure, leaving enough time to accommodate travel delays. Check the route, distance, and travel time. If you forget to verify date, time, and place (including floor and suite

number), you might not even arrive at the right place or on the right day for your interview.

Write it all down legibly and put it with the rest of your interview kit. To arrive at an interview too early indicates overanxiousness, and to arrive late is inconsiderate, so arrive at the interview on time, but at the location early. This allows you time to visit the restroom (usually your only private sanctuary at an interview) and make the necessary adjustments to your appearance, review any notes, and put on your game face. Remember to add contact numbers to your interview kit, so if you are delayed on the way to the interview, you can call and let the interviewer know.

On Arrival at the Interview

When you get to the interview site, visit the restroom to check your appearance and take a couple of minutes to do the following:

- Review the company dossier.
- Review your TJD and resume. Become your resume. Recall your commitment to the profession and the team, and the *transferable skills* and *professional values* that help you succeed.
- Turn off your cell phone: Nothing in the world is more important than this interview, and nothing in the world annoys an interviewer more than your phone ringing or you looking furtively at texts.
- Breathe deeply and slowly for a minute to dispel your natural physical tension.
- During the interview, you can review the list of questions you developed, but it helps get your *head in the zone* to review them now.
- Smile and head for the interview—you are as ready as you are ever going to be.

Under no circumstances should you back out because you do not like the receptionist or the look of the office—that would be allowing personal insecurities to triumph. You are here to improve your most critical professional skill—your ability to turn interviews into job offers; whatever happens, *you can and must learn from this experience.*

Do:
- Give a firm handshake—respond to the interviewer's grip and duration.
- Make eye contact and smile. Say, "Hello, Ms. Larsen. I am John Jones. I've been looking forward to meeting you."

Do Not:
- Use first names (unless asked)
- Smoke (even if invited)
- Sit down (until invited)
- Show anxiety or boredom
- Look at your watch
- Discuss politics, sex, race, national origin, religion, or age
- Show samples of your work (unless requested)
- Ask about benefits, salary, or vacation

Now you're ready for anything—except for the tough questions that are going to be thrown at you next. You've done all your homework: You've studied the building blocks of a successful professional persona and completed the crucial TJD process (Chapters 1–3); you've learned how to take control of your physical appearance and conduct and turn them into an asset (Chapters 5 and 6); and now you've prepared a kit so as never to be caught unawares on the big day. Now, at last, you're ready to do what you came to this book to do: Learn how to answer those tough interview questions. There are lots of them in the following chapters, but all the prep work you've done has instilled in you an underlying familiarity with the logic of professionalism that will make the task much easier. You won't be so much memorizing answers as understanding how the questions aim to evaluate your professional *skills* and *values*, and in the process determine the quality of your *professional persona*.

PART THREE

At the Interview

CHAPTER 8

WHY INTERVIEWERS DO
THE THINGS THEY DO

SITTING IN FRONT OF THE INTERVIEWER as he looks over your resume, your mind racing with the possibilities of what could happen next, you're probably thinking, "This is crazy. Why am I here? I'd rather be abducted by aliens." What probably won't occur to you is that quite a lot of the time the interviewer feels the same way.

There is no getting around the fact that job interviews are scary events, but you are already way ahead of many other candidates because you are seriously investing yourself in developing that critical skill of turning job interviews into job offers.

On the other side of the desk is not an adversary but someone who really would like to hire you. You know that the interviewer you are facing hates to interview. I guarantee that secretly she is thinking, "Please god let this be the one, so I can get back to that pile of work on my desk." You just have to help them make the right decision.

In this part of the book, you'll get right inside the interviewer's head to understand why interviewers do the things they do. And you'll learn the formulas for answering tough interview questions in ways that are honest, unique to you, and advance your candidacy without making you sound like a snake oil salesman.

There's a mistaken belief that any person, on being promoted into the ranks of management, becomes mystically endowed with all the skills of management, including the ability to interview and hire the right people. This is a fallacy; perhaps only half of all managers have been taught how to interview. Most just bumble along and pick up a certain proficiency over time. Consequently, at any job interview you are quite likely to run into one of two types of interviewer:

1. The untrained interviewer who doesn't know what he is doing, and worse, *doesn't know* he doesn't know what he is doing.
2. The competent interviewer who knows exactly what she is doing and has a plan for the interview.

They both present challenges—and opportunities, when you know how to handle them.

Strategies for Interacting with the Untrained Interviewer

Do you ever remember leaving an interview and feeling that you could do the job, but that the interviewer didn't ask you the questions that would allow you to showcase your skills? You were probably facing an untrained interviewer, someone who doesn't know that he doesn't know how to interview, and who bases hiring decisions on "experience" and "knowing people" and "gut feeling."

Facing an untrained interviewer, you must understand how she thinks if you want to turn the situation to your advantage. Untrained interviewers reveal themselves in six distinct ways.

1. The interviewer's desk is cluttered, and he can't find the resume or application that was handed to him a few minutes before.

   Response: Sit quietly through the bumbling and searching. Check out the surroundings. Breathe deeply and slowly to calm any lingering interview nerves. As you bring your adrenaline under control, you bring a calming tone to the interview and the interviewer.

2. The interviewer experiences constant interruptions from the telephone or people walking into the office.

    Response: Interruptions provide opportunities to review what's been happening and plan points you want to make; it's a good time to review the list of questions you want to ask. The interruptions also give you time to think through a question that has just been asked or to add new information to a point made prior to the interruption.

    When an interruption occurs, make a note on your pad of where you were in the conversation and refresh the interviewer on the point when conversation resumes. She will be impressed with your level head and good memory.

3. The interviewer starts with an explanation of why you are both sitting there, and then wanders into a lengthy lecture about the job and/or the company. This interviewer is nervous and doesn't know how to ask questions.

    Response: Show interest in the company and the conversation. Sit straight, look attentive, make appreciative murmurs, and nod at the appropriate times until there is a pause. When that occurs, comment that you appreciate the background on the company, because you can now see more clearly how the job fits into the overall scheme of things and how valuable this or that skill would be for the job. Could the interviewer please tell you some of the other job requirements?

    This is now an interview that you can guide without the interviewer feeling you have taken control of the proceedings. All you have to do is ask the questions from your list. They will demonstrate a real grasp of what is at the heart of this job; the interviewer will be impressed by the grasp of the job that your questions demonstrate.

    Use questions like these: "Would it be of value if I described my experience with _____?" or "Then my experience in

_____ should be a great help to you," or "I recently completed an accounting project just like that. Would it be relevant
to discuss it?"

4. The interviewer begins with, or quickly breaks into, the draw-
   backs of the job. The job may even be described in totally negative terms. That is often done without giving a balanced view of
   the duties and expectations of the position. This usually means
   that the interviewer has had bad experiences hiring for the
   position.

   Response: Listen, then ask why some people fail in this job. The
   interviewer's answers tell you exactly how to sell yourself for this
   position. Address each of the stated negatives and ask what kind
   of person handles this best. Then illustrate your proficiency in
   that particular aspect of the job with a short example from your
   work history.

5. The interviewer keeps asking closed-ended questions—
   questions that demand no more than a yes-or-no answer and
   offer little opportunity to establish your skills. Now, every other
   candidate is facing the same problem, so if you can finesse the
   situation, your candidacy will really stand out.

   Response: The trick is to treat each closed-ended question as if
   the interviewer has added, "Please give me a brief yet thorough
   answer." Closed-ended questions are often mingled with statements followed by pauses. In those instances, agree with the
   statement in a way that demonstrates both a grasp of your job
   and the interviewer's statement. For example: "That's an excellent point, Mr. Smith. I couldn't agree more that the attention
   to detail you describe naturally affects cost containment. My
   track record in this area is . . ."

6. You can also run into "situationally incompetent interviewers,"
   usually when a hiring manager asks colleagues or team members for evaluations without detailing the deliverables of the job

clearly. This problem can be compounded when such interviewers do not know how to interview.

Response: Always take additional copies of your resume with you to the interview to aid extra interviewers in focusing on the appropriate job functions. Be ready to hold up your end of the conversation by asking intelligent questions, the answers to which will enable you to sell your candidacy.

Strategies for Interacting with the Trained Interviewer

A manager's job is to get work done through others, and the first step is to hire the right people. If you cannot hire effectively, you can never manage productively; and if you can't manage productively . . . you lose your job. Consequently, more and more managers are learning how to interview effectively. You can also rely on just about all headhunters, corporate recruiters, and HR people to run competent interviews because it's what they do every day.

Competent interviewers have a plan: They know what they are going to ask, when they are going to ask it, why they are asking it, and what they hope to find. They follow a set format for the interview process to ensure objectivity in the selection process, and a set sequence of questions to ensure the facts are gathered logically and in the right areas. They have all been in many more interviews than you have. We gain three pointers from this:

- You don't need to exaggerate or fabricate: What you have to say is going to capture their full attention; besides, they can tell fact from fiction and truth from dreams.
- You don't need to be uptight or stiff; try to relax and become the friendly, competent, outgoing person you are on your best days. Just don't be a wise-ass.
- This is a job: It needs to be completed so the interviewers can go on to the next one. They are hoping, praying, that you will be the one.

Competent interviewers always have a plan for the interview, and this is what it looks like from the other side of the desk:

How interviews are organized

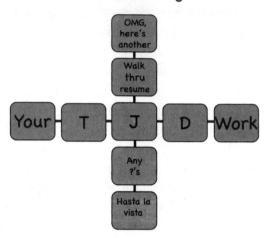

"OMG, Here's Another One"

Yes, that's the first thought in the interviewer's mind as you sit down to begin the interview. It continues, "I pray to the baby Jesus that this is the one. All I want is someone who 'gets' the job, can do it and wants to do it, comes to work on a regular basis, and gets on with people. I just need to hire someone and get back to the emergencies on my desk!"

Contrary to what you may think, *the interviewer wants you to relax.* That's because a more relaxed you is a more communicative you, and the interviewer needs information on which to base her decision. So at the beginning of an interview, you'll move through some formulaic small talk and the offer of a beverage to pave the way for the actual questioning to begin. Always accept the beverage, and ask for water. You *are* nervous, your throat is more prone to dryness, and water is the best remedy.

The interview gets underway with a statement from the interviewer, who will say something along the lines of "We're looking for a _____ , and I want to find out about your experience and the strengths you can bring to our team." He will then explain a bit about how the interview itself will go: whether you'll be talking to other people and if so, who they are. This is the time for you to offer a nicely formatted version of your resume printed on decent paper, because next the interviewer is going to glance down at the resume, and say, "So tell me a little bit about yourself . . ."

Walk Through Your Resume

Using your resume as a reference point, interviewers will often have you walk through your work history, asking you questions about different aspects of your experience. These early questions are designed to get you comfortable with talking, so they will mostly be straightforward, since a good interviewer wants to limit her contributions to about 20 percent of the interview, leaving you to talk the other 80 percent of the time—offering plenty of time to analyze your answers. Your answers should be similarly straightforward, and you'll make an effort here to show an understanding, in general terms, of your job's role within the department, and that in essence the job is about *problem identification, prevention, and solution.*

Some interviews end after this journey through the resume, either because the interviewer has enough information to rule you out, or because he doesn't know any better. Skilled interviewers use this walk through the resume as a qualifying round. If you pass, they'll take the interview to the next level.

Your TJD Work Pays Off

Next the interviewer, examining your resume, will want to look at your qualifications and experience in each of the critical deliverables of the job. Since you already invested time in working back and forth among the job description you're interviewing for, your TJD document, and your resume, you will be able to connect real-world experiences to the *problems anticipated, prevented, and solved* in each area by the intelligent application of the appropriate *technical* and *transferable skills.*

If you make the time to do this, you will be able to connect any question or issue the interviewer raises to the qualifications you bring to the table and illustrate them with real-world examples, explaining:

- What you did and why you did it
- The underlying *transferable skills* you used to get it done
- The *professional values* that helped you make the right judgment calls
- What you learned and how you grew professionally from the experience

Any Questions?

You know the interview is drawing to a close when you are asked if you have any questions. I suggested you make a list of such questions. Bringing out the list and asking what hasn't yet been covered demonstrates the kind of *intelligent enthusiasm* that, again, helps set you apart from other candidates. The list you develop for your first interview can be the template for all subsequent interviews. You will find an extensive list of questions that will demonstrate your intelligent enthusiasm in Chapter 17.

Facing an Interview Panel

There will be situations where you will face more than one interviewer at a time. When these occur, remember the example of an attorney who had five law partners all asking questions at the same time. As the poor interviewee got halfway through one answer, another question would be shot at her. Pausing for breath, she smiled and said, "Hold on, ladies and gentlemen. These are all excellent questions, and, given time, I'll answer them all. Now I believe the managing partner has a question?" In so doing, she showed the interviewers exactly what they wanted to see—someone who remains calm and can function efficiently in stressful situations.

You never know when an interview can take a more stressful turn. It might appear that way because you are tense and tired (remember, it's okay to ask for a restroom break, to recharge yourself, at any time during a day of interviews); or it can be that rubber-stamp meeting with the senior vice president at the end of a series of grueling meetings. That is not surprising. While other interviewers are concerned with determining whether you are able, willing, and a good fit for the job in question, the senior executive who eventually throws you for a loop may be looking at your promotion potential.

Interviewers have developed a number of techniques for throwing you for a loop. The first, and most prominent, is behavioral interviewing.

How to Handle Behavioral Interview Strategies

Behavioral interviewing has become an integral part of almost every job interview today. It is based on the reasonable premise that your past behavior can predict your future performance: "If I know how you behaved in specific situations on someone else's payroll, I'll know how you will behave on mine." To get this insight, an interviewer examines your behavior in general work situations—"Are you comfortable with your accounts receivable skills?"—then looks for examples: "Tell me about a time when you had a problem with an account."

Behavioral interviewing also looks for balance. If the interviewer is feeling impressed, he will try to temper a positive response with, "Great, now tell me about a time when things didn't work out so well." Fortunately, you prepared for this line of questioning when you completed TJD exercises earlier.

How to Handle Stress Interview Strategies

While every job interview is a stress interview, if the ability to function under stress is part of your job—for example, if you work in sales—then the interviewer might reasonably be expected to try to create a temporary environment that reveals how you perform under stress; she is most likely to do this with questions or demands, for example:

"Sell me this pen."

"What would you say if I told you your presentation was lousy?"

"I'm not sure you're right for this job."

Whenever you feel stress rising in an interview, stay calm:

- Breathe evenly and calmly. Shortness of breath will inhibit your thinking process and make you sound nervous.
- If you are offered a beverage at the beginning of the interview, always accept some water. Then if, at any time, you need a moment to collect your thoughts, you can take a sip; besides buying you time to think, swallowing helps reduce any tension you might be feeling.
- Keep your body posture relaxed and open. Many people have a tendency, when under stress, to contract their bodies. This adds to the tension and sends the wrong message.
- Think through the question. Consciously remove any perceived intimidating verbal inflection. For example, depending on the tone of voice used, the question, "I'm not sure you are right for the job. What do you think?" can be heard as, "You just aren't right for this job." Or you could hear it as, "I'd like to hire you and you're one of my top candidates, but I'm not *sure* you're the one, so please convince me."

How to Handle Situational Interview Strategies

Situational strategies give the interviewer an opportunity to see you in something close to a real work situation, with the goal of getting a better idea of how you perform your duties. The situational strategy will always relate to a frequently executed task, something at the very heart of your job, and it can happen as a formal part of the interview or very casually.

Customer service and sales jobs are prone to situational interviewing strategies more than most; if you face one of these, you'll panic a little, but the situational role play is going to recreate a task or situation that is at the core of your work, so try to relax. Ask a few questions for clarification and to get nerves under control. If it's going to take more than a few minutes, you can ask for a restroom break. Then, as much as you can, relax, step up, and do your job. Remember, what is being sought is confirmation that you understand the building blocks of the task: You aren't expected to deliver an Oscar-worthy performance.

Hasta la Vista, Baby

The interviewer will thank you for your time and may give you some idea of next steps. If this information isn't offered, ask for it. If there is another round of interviews, recap:

- Your understanding of the job
- What you bring to the table
- That you are qualified and very interested
- Ask to schedule the next interview

If there are no more interviews, ask when the decision will be made. Then repeat the steps above, but instead of asking for the next interview, ask for the job. You have everything to gain and nothing to lose; showing *motivation* and *intelligent enthusiasm* for the job now could be the decisive factor.

Now that you have a good idea of how the interview will play out, as well as the types of interviewers you will meet and the tactics they will use, it's time to look at the questions that will be heading your way and how to handle them.

CHAPTER 9

HOW TO KNOCK 'EM DEAD: GREAT ANSWERS TO TOUGH INTERVIEW QUESTIONS

ONE OF THE TWO BAD SEATS AT A JOB INTERVIEW is sitting in front of the interviewer wondering what she is going to ask next; the other is sitting across from a candidate wondering what kind of phony, pre-packaged platitudes you are going to be fed in response to a serious question.

All any interviewer really wants is to find someone who can do the job, wants to do the job, and can get along with others. All you need to do to win the job offer is show the interviewer you are that person. You don't need to be phony in your responses: You are the real deal and the interviewer's questions will give you the opportunities to show it.

Fortunately, you are in a position to do this. You know exactly who gets hired for this job and why. Your TJD work revealed how employers prioritize their requirements and how they express them. You determined the experience and skills you possess in each of the deliverable areas of the job, you developed examples of assignments that show you tackling that area's typical problems successfully, and you created behavioral profiles of the person everyone wants to work with and the person nobody wants as an employee. All this is supported by the understanding you gained of how each of the *transferable skills* and *professional values* impacts the responsibilities of the target job and every aspect of your daily professional life. Showing these universally admired *skills* and *values* in your actions gives your answers substance and a ring of truth.

Armed with this knowledge, you are already better prepared than the vast majority of other candidates. Apart from a healthy and perfectly natural case of preperformance nerves, the only rational worry you have left is fear of the unknown: not knowing what questions you might be asked, what is behind them, and how to answer them. That will be our focus for the next few chapters.

I will help you understand what is behind each question—the kind of information an employer is likely to be seeking—and I'll give you examples of the points you should make in your answers. But remember, these are sample answers; they are meant to reveal the logic of the questions and point the way toward answers that work for you.

As you read through the questions and begin to think about what's motivating them, you will see a logical pattern emerge that will help you think through what you can say about your own experience.

Common Opening Questions

There is a very high probability that the first two questions you'll face will be: "Tell me a little about yourself" and "What do you know about the company?" As these questions frequently occur in both telephone and face-to-face interviews, we dealt with them in the telephone interview chapter; to refresh your memory about how to handle them, go back and reread the answers in Chapter 4. Answer these questions well, and you create a good first impression and set the tone for your candidacy.

Why have you been out of work so long?

This question always has you scrambling for an answer; it touches a raw spot and can be humiliating, but you can turn it around by facing and using the facts of the matter.

The facts are that you are a hardworking, competent professional who had always been led to believe that was enough. You'd never had a problem finding work before and no one had ever told you there were specific job search skills you needed to develop, not at home, school, college, or anywhere.

Then you got sideswiped by the biggest recession in eighty years and on top of this, the sudden move to Internet-based recruitment (while you were working and not paying attention to such things) had changed all the rules of job search anyway.

You might try something along the lines of, "If you look at my work history, you'll see it has been steady for _____ years. Then I lost my job. The big problem for me was my complete lack of understanding about how to find a job in the worst recession in eighty years, at a time when recruitment had moved entirely online and changed all the rules of job search.

"I'd never had a problem finding a job before, but because of the changes in how you find a job today, when I did apply for jobs, most of the time my resume got stuck in a database and was never even seen by recruiters. I didn't understand that my resume had to be written differently. The big reason I've been out of work is that my resume didn't work in this new environment and I just haven't been getting interviews."

Then move the conversation forward to what's most important to the interviewer: what you can do and how long it will take you to be productive. You might finish with a question of your own, asking about the most difficult and/or urgent responsibilities of the job and why people fail in this job, "but put me to work and I'll get right back to doing what I do best: identifying, preventing, and solving problems. What are some of the recurring problems your people have to deal with in this job?" The interviewer's answer should give you ammunition to talk about how well-suited you will be for the position.

Your answer should emphasize that while you may not have been in the corporate workplace, neither have you been idle. Talk about how you have kept current with classes or part-time work, and/or what you have been doing to keep the specific *technical skills* of the job honed.

You can also talk about how you used other *transferable skills* and applied *professional values* in whatever work you were doing, noting that these skills are fresh, current, and needed in every job.

> ### Walk me through your job changes. Why did you leave/want to leave this job?

This question comes early in an interview and helps the interviewer understand the chronology and reasoning behind your career moves and gaps in employment. Don't worry about gaps; everyone has to deal with them. You must be ready to walk through your resume without hesitation, making two statements about each employer:

1. What you learned from that job that applies to this one; in other words, the experience you gained from past jobs is an indicator of how you will perform in this one.
2. Why you left. You should have an acceptable reason for leaving every job you have held. The following LAMPS acronym identifies acceptable reasons for leaving a company:

- **L**ocation: The commute was unreasonably long.
- **A**dvancement: You weren't able to grow professionally in that position, either because there were others ahead of you or there was no opportunity for growth.
- **M**oney: You were underpaid for your skills and contribution.
- **P**ride or prestige: You wanted to be with a better company.
- **S**ecurity: The company was not stable.

For example: "My last company was a family-owned affair. I had gone as far as I was able to go. It just seemed time for me to join a more prestigious company and accept greater challenges."

Under no circumstances should you badmouth a manager—even if she was a direct descendant of Attila the Hun. Doing so will only raise a red flag in the interviewer's mind: "Will he be complaining about me like this in a few months?"

This is a "checkbox" question: The interviewer wants to ask the question, check the box, and move on. You get into trouble with too much information. Any answer longer than two short sentences is too long. Use a phrase from the LAMPS acronym above, keep it short and simple, and then shut up; if the interviewer wants more, she will ask.

Why have you changed jobs so frequently?

If you have been caught in mergers and layoffs, simply explain. If you have jumped around, blame it on youth (even the interviewer was young once). Now you realize what a mistake your job-hopping was, and with your added domestic responsibilities you are now much more settled. Or you may wish to impress on the interviewer that your job-hopping was never as a result of poor performance and that you grew professionally as a result of each job change.

You could reply: "My first job had a long commute. I soon realized that, but I knew it would give me good experience in a very competitive field. Subsequently, I found a job much closer to home where the commute was only half an hour each way. I was very happy at my second job. However, I got an opportunity to really broaden my experience base with a new company that was just starting up. With the wisdom of hindsight, I realize that move was a mistake; it took me six months to realize I couldn't make a contribution there. I've been with my current company a reasonable length of time. So I have broad experience in different environments. I didn't just job-hop; I have been following a path to gain broad experience. So you see, I have more experience than the average person of my years, and a desire to settle down and make it pay off for me and my employer."

Or you can say: "Now I want to settle down and make my diverse background pay off in my contributions to my new employer. I have a strong desire to contribute and I am looking for an employer that will keep me challenged; I think this might be the company to do that. Am I right?"

What aspects of your work do you consider most crucial?

All jobs exist to support profitability; you need to determine whether your job is chiefly concerned with generating revenue, protecting assets, improving productivity in some way, or is perhaps a combination of these imperatives. Once you have determined this, you have the framework for an answer.

But to answer effectively, you need to grasp the true guts of your job, which is to *identify, prevent, and solve problems* that occur within your area of expertise, and in the process to *help your employer achieve and maintain profitability.*

Your answer begins with an explanation of why the job exists and what role it plays in achieving departmental and company goals. Then itemize the most important responsibilities of the job (you prioritized these in your TJD).

You then proceed to address:

- The *technical skills* you need to deliver on these responsibilities: "I need to be able to do _____to execute my responsibilities."
- "Of course, crucial to the job is my ability to *identify, prevent, and solve* the problems that crop up in each of these areas every day . . ."
  - (A) You anticipate the ways that problems can arise in your area of responsibility and explain how you execute your work in ways that prevent many of the problems typical to your job from arising in the first place. You have an example or two ready.
  - (B) You tackle and solve problems that do occur, because they cannot be prevented, in a timely, effective, and professional manner. You'll have an illustration ready for this too.

  You do this in a way that is courteous to customers and vendors and considerate to those coworkers who, in their jobs, must deal with the results of your work. Again, you'll have examples.
- Finally, make mention of one or two of the *transferable skills* and *professional values* that help you deliver on these crucial responsibilities: "So my *multitasking, communication,* and *critical thinking skills* help me do this every day . . ."

the damn thing over. It is important that your answer show that you remain objective and don't take shortcuts.

Tell me about a time things went wrong.

You are asked to talk about something that went wrong, but that doesn't mean you can't do so with an example that turned out fine. Your TJD identified a number of examples you can use. Choose an example and paint it black, but don't point the finger of blame; crap happens.

End with how you solved the problem or contributed to its solution. Get in a subtle plug for *transferable skills*: ". . . so sticking with it and doing it by the book helped us put things right in the end."

You can go on to explain that the next time you faced the same kind of problem you had a better frame of reference, knew what to avoid, what to do more of, and what other new approaches you could try. Finish your answer with a statement about what you learned.

How have you benefited from your disappointments/mistakes?

You learn more from failures, mistakes, and errors than you do from successes, so this is an opportunity for you to demonstrate your *emotional maturity* (you stay calm) and *critical thinking skills* (you think things through objectively).

Your answer will explain how you treat setbacks as learning experiences: You look at what happened, why it happened, and how you can do things differently at each stage. Edison once explained his success as an inventor by claiming that he knew more ways *not* to do something than anyone else living; you can do worse than to quote him. In any event, sum up your answer with, "I treat disappointments as a learning experience. I look at what happened, why it happened, and how I would do things differently in each stage should the same set of circumstances appear again. That way, I put disappointment behind me and am ready with renewed vigor and understanding to face the new day's problems."

You don't need to be specific about your failures, but be prepared with an example in case of a follow-up question starting, "Tell me about a time when . . ."

What are you looking for in your next job?

Ask not what your company can do for you; ask what you can do for your company. You are there to get a job offer, and you only want to address your needs when an offer is on the table and negotiation likely.

With so little real knowledge about the company, you need to be careful about specificity. Keep your answer general and focus on the fulfillment you experience from a job well done, with a team similarly committed, working for a company with a solid reputation. If you're lower on the success ladder, add learned and earned professional growth to this—although if your future boss is the next step up . . . not such a good idea. You can add that you have observed that good people seem to move forward in groups and you'd like to earn a place within this inner circle and earn the opportunity to grow as circumstances allow by making a consistent difference with your presence.

What do you spend most of your time on, and why?

Your answer obviously needs to show that you focus on top priorities, and you can make additional points by noting that you don't ignore the important but time-consuming repetitive tasks. You can mention some small thing that has to be done frequently, because if it has to be done frequently, it is obviously critical to success. But don't do this at the expense of those top priorities, or you're likely to be pegged as someone who gets bogged down in minutiae.

Another tactic is to use an example of *multitasking* to emphasize how you manage the priorities of the job. For example, "Like a lot of businesspeople, I work on the telephone and meetings take up a great deal of time. What's important to me is prioritization of activities based on the deliverables of my job. I find more gets achieved in a shorter time if a meeting is scheduled, say, immediately before lunch or at the close of business. I try to block my time in the morning and the afternoon for main-thrust activities. At four o'clock, I review what I've achieved, what went right or wrong, and plan adjustments and my main thrust for tomorrow."

What are your qualifications for this job?

The interviewer is interested in your experience and your possession of the *technical skills* to do the job, your academic qualifications, and the *transferable skills/professional values* that enable you to do any task well. This is why you need a clear recall of which *transferable skills* help you execute each aspect of your job.

When you are confident in your skills, you can learn more about the job and make points for your candidacy by asking a question of your own: "If you could tell me about specific work assignments I'll be involved with early on, I can show exactly how I can make real contributions in this job."

What can you do for us that someone else cannot do?

You cannot know other candidates' capabilities, so smilingly disarm your interviewer with this fact, then say, "But what I bring is . . ." Your answer will then demonstrate your grasp of the job's responsibilities, the problems that occur in each area, and how you are prepared to deal with them.

You can finish your answer with reference to the *transferable skills* and *professional values* you bring to the job: "I also bring to this job a *determination* to see projects through to a proper conclusion. I *listen* and take direction well. I am *analytical* and don't jump to conclusions. I understand we are in business to make a *profit*, so I keep an eye on cost and return." End with: "How do these qualifications fit your needs?" or "What else are you looking for?" If you haven't covered the interviewer's hot buttons, she will cover them now, and you can respond accordingly.

How do you stay current?

We live in an age of technological innovation, in which the nature of every job is changing as quickly as you turn these pages. This means you must look to professional education as the price of sustained employability. In your answer, talk about the importance of keeping abreast of changes in the profession. You can refer to:

- Courses you have taken or are planning to take
- Books you have read or are reading
- Membership in professional associations
- Subscriptions to professional journals or online groups you belong to

If you're not already doing some of these things, you need to start *now*.

What achievements are you most proud of?

Use an example of something that is at the core of your job and central to its success, where you were part of a team working on some larger project beyond the scope of individual contribution, or where you accepted responsibility for some dirty/ignored project that nevertheless had importance to the success of your department. Don't exaggerate your contributions to major projects—share the success and be seen as a *team player*. Be honest, and to guarantee your illustrations are relevant, take them from your TJD. For example: "Although I feel my biggest achievements are still ahead of me, I am proud of my involvement with _____. I made my contribution as part of that team and learned a lot in the process."

Tell me about the most difficult project you've tackled.

The interviewer wants to know
(A) you have experience relative to current projects
(B) How you handle them

When possible, discuss projects that parallel work you are likely to do at the new job. State the project, then identify its challenges (in some detail), your *critical thinking* process to isolate causes of the problem and possible solutions, the story of your implementation of the solution, and the value it delivered to your employer.

Tell me about an important goal you set recently.

Your answer should cite a goal that relates to productivity or another aspect related to the more important deliverables of your job in some way. You might use a skill-development goal, explaining why you chose it, how it helped you grow, and the benefits of completion. Or you can talk about a productivity/performance standard goal, why you chose it, and how it helped. You can add to this how you integrated achieving this goal into all your other activities, which allows you to talk about your *multitasking skills.*

What have you done to become more effective in your job?

Similarly to the prior question, behind this is an interest in your *motivation* to do the work being offered. The interviewer is looking for a fit between your dreams and her reality.

All worthwhile jobs require hard work and a desire to learn. Technology changes mean your job skills must always be in development if you want to remain current and viable. The interviewer wants to know if you are *committed* to your profession, and is looking for *at least* one example. You can also talk of the mentor relationships you have formed, the books and professional commentaries you've read, the professional organizations you belong to, the certifications you're earning, the courses you are enrolled in, and the webinars you attend. If you aren't doing some of these things, wake up and start *now.*

How do you rank among your peers?

The interviewer is examining your self-esteem. In some cases (for instance in sales) it may be possible for you to quantify this: "I'm number two in the region." In other cases, you'll be more subjective, but you should strive to be realistic. You might slip in a real-life detail such as, "There are two groups in my department: those who make a difference, and those who watch. I'm in the first group."

Your answer should illustrate a commitment to productivity and professional development. Explain how you ensure that your work is executed effectively and, if you can, cite endorsements given you by managers. You see each day as an opportunity to learn and contribute, and you see the environment at this company as conducive to your best efforts. Perhaps say something like, "Given the parameters of my job, my progress has been excellent. I know the work, and I am just reaching that point in my career where I can make significant contributions."

You might finish by saying that being at this interview means you've gone as far as you can with your present employer and that this environment at _____ and its new ways will encourage a new spurt of growth.

If you hope to get ahead in your professional life, any job you ever hold will every now and then deliver opportunities to reschedule your personal life and otherwise mess up your weekends. But these invasions of personal time are nevertheless opportunities to show your *commitment* and *team spirit*, so you always step up when these sometimes unwelcome opportunities present themselves; doing so increases professional success . . . and that gives you better personal time. Answer "Yes," and then illustrate with a story of making extra and special efforts with good humor.

Tell me about a time when an emergency caused you to reschedule your workload/projects.

The question examines *multitasking skills* and how you handle emergency imperatives. You'll make points when you explain how your *planning* and *time-management skills* help you stay on top of your regular responsibilities even when emergency priorities throw normal scheduling off.

The story you then tell should illustrate your flexibility and willingness to work extra hours when necessary. Demonstrate that your *multitasking skills* allow you to change course without having a nervous breakdown.

How long will it take you to make a contribution?

It takes time to understand *systems and procedures*, who the power players are, and why things are done the way they are. Be sure to qualify the question: In what area does the interviewer need rapid contributions? You might ask, "Where are your greatest areas of need right now?" You give yourself time to think while the interviewer explains priorities.

What is the most difficult situation you have faced?

You're really being asked two different questions: "What do you consider difficult?" and "How did you handle it?" This means the interviewer will be evaluating both your *critical thinking* and *technical skills*.

Don't talk about problems with coworkers. Instead, focus on a job-related problem. Throughout the book, we have talked about the importance of problem solving and the steps a professional takes to identify the most appropriate approaches and solutions; you should have numerous examples from your TJD with which to illustrate your answer. Make sure to identify the benefits of your solution.

What do you think determines progress in a good company?

The interviewer needs to see that you understand progress is earned over time and does not come as a result of simply showing up to work on a regular basis. Begin with each of the *technical skills* required to do the job, briefly citing the *transferable skills* that allow you to do the job well. Finish with your *willingness* to take the rough with the smooth that goes with every job, and the good fortune of having a manager who wants you to succeed.

What are some of the problems you encounter in doing your job, and what do you do about them?

There's a trap in this question and two areas you need to cover in your response, so your answer has three steps:

1. First the trap: Note well the old saying, "A poor workman blames his tools," and don't find problems with the job itself or the tools you have to execute that job. Next, the two areas you need to cover:

2. Whatever your title, at its heart your job is about *problem identification, prevention, and solution.* Make this statement with details of the problems you are a specialist in preventing and solving. This part of your answer demonstrates your deep understanding of your work.

3. Your awareness that careless mistakes cost the company good money means you are always on the lookout for potential problems caused by oversight. For example: "Some parts of my job are fairly repetitive, so it's easy to overlook problems. Lots of people do. However, I always look for them; it helps keep me alert and motivated, so I do a better job. To give you an example, we make computer-memory disks. Each one has to be machined by hand, and, once completed, the slightest abrasion will turn one into a reject. I have a steady staff and little turnover, and everyone wears cotton gloves to handle the disks. Yet about six months ago, the reject rate suddenly went through the

roof. Is that the kind of problem you mean? Well, the cause was one that could have gone unnoticed for ages. Jill, the section head who inspects all the disks, had lost a lot of weight, and her diamond engagement ring was slipping around her finger, scratching the disks as she passed them and stacked them to be shipped. Our main client was giving us a big problem over it, so my looking for problems and paying attention to detail really paid off."

In your last job, how did you plan to interview?

If you are a manager, getting work done through others is at the very heart of your job. Recruitment and selection are part of your job description, and you can expect this question. Your answer should give a description of how the skilled interviewer prepares, as we discussed in Chapter 8. You might also read *Hiring the Best* and the e-book *Knock 'em Dead Breaking Into Management: The Essentials of Survival & Success* (details at *www.knockemdead.com*).

If I hired you today, what would you accomplish first?

Gear your answer to first getting settled in the job, understanding how things are done, and becoming a member of the team. You would mention that of course this includes a clear priority on all your responsibilities. Then finish with a question, "What are the most critical projects/problems you'll want me to tackle?" The response to that becomes your final answer to what you will accomplish first.

What type of decisions do you make in your work?

This examines the extent of your authority and how *critical thinking* enters into your work. With the TJD, you will have a clear understanding of the job's deliverables and can determine the decision-making events that are integral to your job. The interviewer will certainly follow up with a request for an example; your answer will address the types of decisions you make and include an example that shows how you approach making them.

How do you handle rejection?

This question is common if you are applying for a job in sales, including face-to-face sales, telemarketing, public relations, and customer service. If you are after a job in one of these areas and you really don't like the heavy doses of rejection that are any salesperson's lot, consider a new field. The anguish you will experience will not lead to a successful career or a happy life.

With that in mind, let's look behind the question. The interviewer simply wants to know whether you take rejection as rejection of yourself or whether you simply accept it as a temporary rejection of a service or product. Here is a sample answer that you can tailor to your particular needs and background: "I accept rejection as an integral part of the sales process. If everyone said 'yes' to a product, there would be no need for the sales function. As it is, I see every rejection as bringing me closer to the customer who *will* say 'yes.' Sales is a profession of communication, determination, and resiliency; rejection is just part of the process, it's nothing personal. I always try to leave the potential customer with a good feeling, as no sale today can well become a sale next month."

Tell me about a situation that frustrated you at work.

This question is about *emotional maturity*. The interviewer wants to know how you channel frustration into productivity. Give an example of a difficult situation in which you remained diplomatic and objective and found a solution that benefited all concerned. Show yourself to be someone who isn't managed by emotions: You acknowledge the frustration, then put it aside in favor of achieving the goals of the job you are paid to do.

What interests you least about this job?

The question is potentially explosive but easily defused. Regardless of your occupation, there is at least one repetitive, mindless duty that everyone groans about but that nevertheless goes with the territory. Use that as your example. "_____are probably the least demanding part of my job. However, I know they are important for _____, so I do them at the end of the day as part of my performance review and next-day planning." Notice how this response also shows that you are *organized* and possess *critical thinking* and *multitasking skills*; it also shows you understand that it is necessary to take the rough with the smooth.

I'm not sure you're suitable for the job (too inexperienced).

In a job search you quickly develop a feeling for whether a particular position is a close match, a job you've already done for so long that you might be perceived as too experienced (too heavy), or a job that might be a bit of a stretch (too light). If you can see a potential problem with an opportunity, the employer probably can too. Nevertheless, you were close enough to get the interview, so make every effort to land the offer.

This could also be used as a stress question (to see how you handle adverse situations, see Chapter 11). The interviewer's "I'm not sure" could really mean, "I'd like to hire you, so here's a wide-open opportunity to sell me on you." Either way, remain calm and accept this as another opportunity to set you apart from other candidates.

Put the ball straight back into the interviewer's court: "Why do you say that?" You need more information and time to organize an appropriate reply, but it is also important to show that you are not intimidated.

When you might be too light, your answer itemizes all the experience and skills you bring, and offsets weaknesses with other strengths and examples of how efficiently you develop new skills.

You can also talk about the motivation you bring to the job, and that you will expect to be motivated for some considerable time because of the opportunity the job offers for your professional development, while someone with all the skills is going to need a quick promotion to keep him happy. You can finish your answer with a reflexive question that encourages a "yes" answer, "Wouldn't you agree?"

I'm not sure you're suitable for the job (too experienced).

If you are told you have too much experience, respond with the positives: how your skills help you deliver immediately, and why the position fits your needs; perhaps, "I really enjoy my work, so I won't get bored, and I'm not looking for a promotion, so I'm not after anyone's job. I'll be a reliable and trustworthy person to have at your back. I have excellent skills [itemize], so I can deliver quickly and consistently. My experience makes me a steadying member of the team, and when you think I'm ready, I can help mentor." Finish with a smile, ". . . and let's not forget, I've already made my mistakes on somebody else's payroll."

Do you have any questions?

A sign that the interview is drawing to a close. Take the opportunity to make a strong impression. Ask questions that help advance your candidacy by giving you information about the real-world experience of the job: "Yes, I do have one or two questions." You might ask:

- Who succeeds in this job and why?
- Who fails in this job and why?
- What are the major projects of the first six months?
- What will you want me to have achieved after ninety days?
- What will you want me to have achieved after six months?
- What will my first assignment be?

For a longer list of the sort of questions you might want to ask, check out Chapter 14.

Most candidates ask questions about money and benefits. These are nice-to-know questions that an interviewer is not really interested in discussing at this point. As your goal at every interview is to bring the interviewer to the point of offering you the job, such questions are really irrelevant because they don't bring you closer to the job offer. Better that you concentrate on gathering information that will help you further your candidacy.

Ask about next steps if there are more interviews. If there are, match your skills to the needs of the job, explain your interest in the job and desire to pursue it; ask for the next interview.

If there's not another interview, cite your understanding of the job, how your skills match each of the deliverables, state that you want the job and want to join the team, and ask for the job.

CHAPTER 10

Questions of Manageability
and Teamwork

"What are you like to work with, Mr. Jones?" Learn the techniques interviewers use to find out if you are manageable, if you will fit in, and most important, whether you are the type of person who is able to work toward common goals and with whom others like to work.

When you join a new company, you will be working with the hiring manager and his team for fifty weeks of the year. Every interviewer, recruiter, manager, and coworker wants to know whether you will fit in with the rest of the staff, whether you are a team player, and most of all, whether you are manageable. Fortunately, you have carefully thought through the behaviors of professional success and failure; and as a result, you have a clear idea of who you are and how you behave professionally. This self-awareness will help you handle the questions addressed in this chapter.

A big part of your job as that small but important cog in the moneymaking machinery of the corporation is to mesh with the other cogs in your department (and beyond) to support those departmental deliverables that are beyond the scope of individual effort. Your being manageable and a team player are significant considerations for hiring managers. Here are the questions your interviewers will ask to assess this.

How do you take direction?

The interviewer wants to know whether you are open-minded and can be a team player. Can you follow directions, or are you a difficult, high-maintenance employee? The employer hopes that you are a low-maintenance professional who is motivated to ask clarifying questions about a project before beginning and who then gets on with the job at hand, coming back with requests for direction as circumstances dictate.

This particular question can also be defined as "How do you accept criticism?" Your answer should cover both points: "I take direction well and recognize that it can come in two varieties, depending on the circumstances. There is carefully explained direction, when my boss has time to lay things out for me in detail; then there are those times when, as a result of deadlines and other pressures, the direction might be brief and to the point. While I have seen some people get upset with that, personally I've always understood that there are probably other considerations I am not aware of. As such, I take the direction and get on with the job without taking offense, so my boss can get on with her job."

Would you like to have your boss's job?

It is a rare boss who wants his livelihood taken away. On my own very first job interview, my future boss said, "Mr. Yate, it has been a pleasure to meet you. However, until you walked in my door, I wasn't out on the street looking for a new job." You see, I had this case of wanting to start at the top rather than actually work my way up.

The interviewer wants to know if you are the type of person who will be confrontational or undermining. She also seeks to determine how goal-oriented and motivated you are in your work life—so you may also want to comment on your sense of direction. But while ambition is admired, it is admired most by those far enough above the fray not to be threatened. Be cautiously optimistic; perhaps, "Well, if my boss were promoted over the coming years, I would hope to have made a consistent enough contribution to warrant his consideration.

It's not that I am looking to take anyone's job; rather, I am looking for a manager who will help me develop my capabilities."

What do you think of your current/last boss?

Be short and sweet and shut up. People who complain about their employers are recognized as the people who cause the most disruption in a department. This question is the interviewer's way of finding out if you're going to cause trouble. "I liked her as a person, respected her professionally, and appreciated her guidance." The question is often followed by one that tries to validate your answer.

Describe a situation where your work or an idea of yours was criticized.

This is a doubly dangerous question because you are being asked to describe how you handle criticism, and to detail inadequacies. If you have the choice, describe a poor idea that was criticized, not poor work.

Put your example in the past, make it small, and show what you learned from the experience. Show that you go through these steps to become maximally productive:

- Listen to understand.
- Confirm the understanding.
- Ask for guidance.
- Confirm the desired outcome.
- Show a satisfactory resolution.
- Address what you learned and how the experience helped you grow.

You might end with something that captures the essence of your example: "I listened carefully and asked a couple of questions for clarification. Then I fed back what I heard to make sure the facts were straight. I asked for advice, we bounced some ideas around, then I came back later and re-presented the idea in a more viable format. My supervisor's input was invaluable." Those are steps you go through to become maximally productive in these situations.

How do you get along with different kinds of people?

You don't have to talk about respect for others, the need for diversity, or how it took you ten years to realize Jane was a different sex and Charley a different color, because that is not what this question is about. If you respect others, you will demonstrate this by explaining to your interviewer how you work in a team environment (because this is, in reality, a "team player" question) and how you solicit and accept input, ideas, and viewpoints from a variety of sources. Give a quick, honest illustration of working productively with a person who is different from you in terms of personality or in terms of the demands their job places on them—and how you respond to maximize productivity and a harmonious work environment.

Rate yourself on a scale of one to ten.

This question is meant to plumb the depths of your self-esteem and self-awareness. If you answer ten, you run the risk of portraying yourself as insufferable. On the other hand, if you say less than seven, you might as well get up and leave. Your best bet is probably an eight: Say that you always give of your best, which includes ongoing personal and professional development, and that in doing so, you always increase your skills and therefore always see room for improvement. It helps to give an example: "I just read a great book on time-management called *How to Get Control of Your Time and Your Life*, and found that a daily plan/do/review cycle is a really useful tool for staying on top of and prioritizing multiple projects."

What kinds of things do you worry about?

Some questions, such as this one, can seem so off-the-wall that you might start treating the interviewer as a confessor in no time flat. Your private phobias have nothing to do with your job, and revealing them can get you labeled as unbalanced. It is best to confine your answer to the sensible worries of a conscientious professional. "I worry about deadlines, staff turnover, tardiness, backup plans for when the computer crashes, or that one of my auditors will burn out or defect to the competition—just the normal stuff. It goes with the territory, so I don't let it get me down." Whatever you identify as a worry might then be the subject of a follow-up question, so think through the worry you state and how you cope with it.

What have you done that shows initiative?

The question probes whether you are a doer, someone who will look for ways to increase revenue and/or productivity—the kind of person who makes a difference for good with her presence every day. Be sure, however, that your example of initiative does not show a disregard for company *systems and procedures*.

The story you tell should show you stepping up to do a necessary job others didn't see as important or didn't want to do. For example, "Every quarter, I sit down with my boss and find out the dates of all her meetings for the next three months. I immediately make the hotel and flight arrangements, and attend to all the web-hosting details. I ask myself questions like, 'If the agenda for the July meeting needs to reach the attendees at least six weeks before the meeting, when must it be finished by?' Then I come up with a deadline. I do that for all the major activities for all the meetings. I put the deadlines in her Blackberry and in mine two weeks earlier to ensure everything is done on time. My boss is the best-organized, most relaxed manager in the company."

If you could make one constructive suggestion to management, what would it be?

What matters here is less the specific content of your answer than the tone. Suggest what you know to be true and what your interviewer will appreciate as a breath of fresh air: Most people want to do a good job. Management should create an environment where striving for excellence is encouraged *and* where those who are "retired on the job" have the opportunity to change their ways or leave. Everyone would benefit.

Why do you feel you are a better_____ than some of your coworkers?

The trick is to answer the question without showing yourself in anything but a flattering light. "I don't spend my time thinking about how I am better than my colleagues, because that would be detrimental to our working together as a team. I believe, however, some of the qualities that make me an outstanding _____ are . . ." From here, go on to itemize specific *technical skills* of your profession in which you are particularly strong, and a couple of the *transferable skills* that apply to doing these aspects of your work so well.

What are some of the things that bother you?/What are your pet peeves?/ Tell me about the last time you felt anger on the job.

It is tremendously important to show you can remain calm. Most of us have seen a colleague lose his cool on occasion—not a pretty sight, and one that every sensible employer wants to avoid. This question comes up more and more often the higher up the corporate ladder you climb and the more frequent your contact with clients and the general public. To answer it, find something that angers conscientious workers. "I enjoy my work and believe in giving value to my employer. Dealing with clock-watchers and people who regularly get sick on Mondays and Fridays really bothers me, but it's not something that gets me angry." An answer of this nature will help you much more than the kind given by one engineer who went on for several minutes about how he hated the small-mindedness of people who don't like pet rabbits in the office.

In what areas do you feel your supervisor could have done a better job?

The same goes for this one. No one admires a Monday-morning quarterback. You could reply, though: "I have always had the highest respect for my supervisor. I have always been so busy learning from Mr. Jones that I don't think he could have done a better job. He has really brought me to the point where I am ready for greater challenges. That's why I'm here."

What are some of the things your supervisor did that you disliked?

If you and the interviewer are both nonsmokers, for example, and your boss isn't, use it. Apart from that: "You know, I've never thought of our relationship in terms of like or dislike. I've always thought our role was to get along together and get the job done."

How well do you feel your boss rated your job performance?

This is one very sound reason to ask for written evaluations of your work before leaving a company. Some performance-review procedures include a written evaluation of your performance—perhaps your company employs it. If you work for a company that asks you to sign your formal review, you are quite entitled to request a copy of it. You should also ask for a letter of recommendation whenever you leave a job: You have nothing to lose. If you don't have written references, perhaps say: "My supervisor always rated my job performance well. In fact, I was always rated as being capable of accepting further responsibilities. The problem was there was nothing available in the company—that's why I'm here."

If you have done your research properly, you can quote verbal appraisals of your performance from prior jobs. "In fact, my boss recently said that I was the most organized engineer in the work group, because . . ."

How do I get the best out of you/did your boss get the best out of you?

The interviewer could be envisioning you as an employee. Encourage the thought by describing a supportive manager who outlined projects and their expected results at the start, noted deadlines, shared her greater experience and perspectives, and told you about potential problems. She always shared the benefit of experience. You agreed on a plan of attack for the work, and how and when you needed to give status updates along the way. Your boss was always available for advice and taught you to take the work seriously but encouraged a collegial team atmosphere.

How interested are you in sports?

The interviewer is looking for your involvement in groups, as a signal that you know how to get along with others and pull together as a team.

"I really enjoy most team sports. I don't get a lot of time to indulge myself, but I am a regular member of my company's softball team." A recently completed survey of middle- and upper-management personnel found that the executives who listed group sports/activities among their extracurricular activities made an average of $3,000 per year more than their sedentary colleagues. Don't you just love baseball suddenly?

Apart from team sports, endurance sports are seen as a sign of determination: Swimming, running, and cycling are all okay. Games of skill (bridge, chess, and the like) demonstrate analytical skills; despite the recent popularity of poker and recognition of it as a game of analytical, math, communication, and negotiation skills, I feel that mentioning poker should be avoided.

What personal characteristics are necessary for success in your field?

You know the answer to this one: It's a brief recital of your *transferable skills* and *professional values*.

You might say: "To be successful in my field? Drive, motivation, energy, confidence, determination, good communication, and analytical skills. Combined, of course, with the ability to work with others." Your answer will be more powerful if you relate *transferable skills* and *professional values* to the prime needs of the job.

Do you prefer working with others or alone?

This question is usually used to determine whether you are a team player. Before answering, however, be sure you know whether the job requires you to work alone. Then answer appropriately. Perhaps: "I'm quite happy working alone when necessary. I don't need constant reassurance. But I prefer to work in a group—so much more gets achieved when people pull together."

Explain your role as a group/team member.

You are being asked to describe yourself as either a team player or a loner. Think for a moment about why the job exists in the first place: It is there to contribute to the bottom line in some way, and as such it has a specific role in the department to contribute toward that larger goal. Your department, in turn, has a similar, but larger, role in the company's bottom line. Your ability to link your small role to that of the department's larger responsibilities, and then to the overall success of the company, will demonstrate a developed professional awareness. Most departments depend on harmonious teamwork for their success, so describe yourself as a team player: "I perform my job in a way that helps others to do theirs in an efficient manner. Beyond the mechanics, we all have a responsibility to make the workplace a friendly and pleasant one, and that means everyone working for the common good and making the necessary personal sacrifices for it."

How would you define a motivational work atmosphere?

This is a tricky question, especially because you probably have no idea what kind of work atmosphere exists in that particular office. The longer your answer, the greater your chances of saying the wrong thing, so keep it short and sweet. "One where the team has a genuine interest in its work and desire to turn out a good product/deliver a good service."

Do you make your opinions known when you disagree with the views of your supervisor?

If you can, state that you come from an environment where input is encouraged when it helps the team's ability to get the job done efficiently. "If opinions are sought in a meeting, I will give mine, although I am careful to be aware of others' feelings. I will never criticize a coworker or a superior in an open forum; besides, it is quite possible to disagree without being disagreeable. However, my last manager made it clear that she valued my opinion by asking for it. So, after a while, if there was something I felt strongly about, I would make an appointment to sit down and discuss it one-on-one."

> ### What would you say about a supervisor who was unfair or difficult to work with?

"I would make an appointment to see the supervisor and diplomatically explain that I felt uncomfortable in our relationship, that I felt he was not treating me as a professional colleague, and therefore that I might not be performing up to standard in some way—that I wanted to right matters and ask for his input as to what I must do to create a professional relationship. I would take responsibility for any communication problems that might exist and make it clear that, just as I took responsibility for the problem, I was also taking responsibility for the solution."

> ### Do you consider yourself a natural leader or a born follower?

Ouch! The way you answer depends a lot on the job offer you are chasing. If you are a recent graduate, you are expected to have high aspirations, so go for it. If you are already on the corporate ladder with some practical experience in the school of hard knocks, you might want to be a little cagier. Assuming you are up for (and want) a leadership position, you might try something like this: "I would be reluctant to regard anyone as a natural leader. Hiring, motivating, and disciplining other adults and at the same time molding them into a cohesive team involves a number of delicately tuned skills that no honest person can say they were born with. Leadership requires first of all the desire; then it is a lifetime learning process. Anyone who reckons they have it all under control and have nothing more to learn isn't doing the employer any favors."

Of course, a little humility is also in order, because just about every leader in every company reports to someone, and there is a good chance that you are talking to just such a someone right now. So you might consider including something like, "No matter how well developed any individual's leadership qualities, an integral part of leadership ability is the ability to take direction from your immediate boss, and also to seek the input of the people being supervised. The wise leader will always follow good advice and sound business judgment, wherever it comes from. I would say that the true leader in the modern business world must embrace both." How can anyone disagree with that kind of wisdom?

> *You have a doctor's appointment at noon. You've waited two weeks to get in. An urgent meeting is scheduled at the last moment, though. What do you do?*

What a crazy question, you mutter. It's not. It is even more than a question—it is what I call a question shell. The question within the shell—in this instance, "Will you sacrifice the appointment or sacrifice your job?"—can be changed at will. This is a situational-interviewing technique, which poses an on-the-job problem to see how the prospective employee will respond. A Chicago company asks this question as part of its initial screening, and if you give the wrong answer, you never even get a face-to-face interview. So what is the right answer to this or any similar shell question?

Fortunately, once you understand the interviewing technique, it is quite easy to handle—all you have to do is turn the question around. "If I were the manager who had to schedule a really important meeting at the last moment, and someone on my staff chose to go to the doctor instead, how would I feel?"

It is unlikely that you would understand unless the visit was for a triple bypass. To answer, you start with an evaluation of the importance of the problem and the responsibility of everyone to make some sacrifices for the organization, and finish with: "The first thing I would do is reschedule the appointment and save the doctor's office inconvenience. Then I would immediately make sure I was properly prepared for the emergency meeting."

> *How do you manage to interview while still employed?*

As long as you don't explain that you faked a dentist appointment to make the interview, you should be all right. Beware of revealing anything that might make you appear at all underhanded. Best to make the answer short and sweet, and let the interviewer move on to richer areas of inquiry. Just explain that you had some vacation time due or took a day off in lieu of overtime payments. "I had some vacation time, so I went to my boss and explained that I needed a couple of days off for some personal business and asked her which days would be most suitable. Although I plan to change jobs, I don't in any way want to hurt my current employer in the process by being absent during a crunch."

How have your career motivations changed over the years?

This question only crops up when you have enough years under your belt to be regarded as a tenured professional. The interviewer's agenda is to examine your *emotional maturity* and how realistic you are about future professional growth.

Your answer requires self-awareness. While the desire to rule the world can be seen as *motivation* in young professionals, it may not be interpreted so positively coming from a tenured corporate soldier from whom more realism is expected.

Your answer should reflect a growing maturity as well as a desire to do a good job for its own sake and to make a contribution as part of the greater whole. Here's an example you can use as a starting point in crafting your own:

"I guess in earlier years I was more ego-driven, with everything focused on becoming a star. Over the years I've come to realize that nothing happens with a team of one—we all have to function as part of a greater whole if we are to make meaningful contributions with our professional presence. Nowadays I take great pleasure in doing a job well, in seeing it come together as it should, and especially in seeing a group of professionals working together in their different roles to make it happen. I've discovered that the best way to stand out is to be a real team player and not worry about standing out."

How do you regroup when things haven't gone as planned?

At times we can all react to adversity in pretty much the same way we did as kids, but that isn't always productive, and it isn't what an interviewer wants to hear. Here's a way you can deal with setbacks in your professional life and wow your interviewer in the process:

"I pause for breath and reflection for as long as the situation allows—this can be a couple of minutes or overnight. I do this to analyze what went wrong and why. I'm also careful to look for the things that went right, too. I'll examine alternate approaches and, time allowing, I'll get together with a peer or my boss and review the whole situation and my proposed new approaches."

You can go on to explain that the next time you face the same kind of problem you'll know what to avoid, what to do more of, and what other new approaches you can try.

You might consider finishing your answer with a statement about the beneficial effects of experiencing problems. "Over the years, I've learned just as much from life's problems as from its successes."

Have you ever had to make unpopular decisions?

Inherent in the question is a request for an example, in which you'll demonstrate how *critical thinking* and *leadership skills* help you make the unpopular decisions, while *teamwork* and *communication skills* help you make them palatable. Your answer needs to show that you're not afraid to make unpopular decisions when they are in the best interests of your job or the department's goals.

Simultaneously, stress your effort to make the decision workable for all parties, and finish by explaining how everyone subsequently accepted its necessity and got on board.

What would your coworkers tell me about your attention to detail?

Say that you are shoddy and never pay attention to the details, and you'll hear a whoosh as your job offer flies out the window.

Your answer obviously lies in the question. You pay attention to detail, your analytical approach to projects helps you identify all the component parts of a given job, and your *multitasking skills* ensure that you get the job done in a timely manner without anything falling through the cracks.

What do you do when there is a decision to be made and no procedure exists?

You need to show that even though you're more than capable of taking initiative, you're not a rogue missile. Explain that the first thing you'll do will be to discuss the situation with your boss or—if time is tight and this isn't possible—with peers. That's exactly what the hiring manager wants to hear. Make clear that in developing any new approach/procedure/idea, you'll stick to the company's established *systems and procedures.*

When do you expect a promotion?

Tread warily. Show you believe in yourself but have both feet firmly planted on the ground. "That depends on a few criteria. Of course, I cannot expect promotions without the performance that marks me as deserving of promotion. I also need to join a company that has the growth necessary to provide the opportunity. I hope that my manager believes in promoting from within, and will help me grow so that I will have the skills necessary to be considered for promotion when the opportunity comes along."

If you are the only one doing a particular job in the company, or you are in management, you need to build another factor into your answer. "As a manager, I realize that part of my job is to have done my succession planning, and that I must have someone trained and ready to step into my shoes before I can expect to step up. That way, I play my part in preserving the chain of command." To avoid being caught off-guard with queries about your having achieved that in your present job, you can finish with: "Just as I have done in my present job, where I have a couple of people capable of taking over the reins when I leave."

Tell me a story.

Wow. What on earth does the interviewer mean by that question? You don't know until you get her to elaborate. Ask, "What would you like me to tell you a story about?" To make any other response is to risk making a fool of yourself. Sometimes the question is asked to evaluate how analytical you are: People who answer the question without qualifying show they do not think things through carefully. It can also be asked to get a glimpse of the things you hold important. The answer you get to your request for clarification may give you direction, or it may not; but either way it demonstrates your *critical thinking skills*.

You need to have a story ready that portrays you in an appropriate light. If you speak of your personal life, tell a story that shows you like people, are engaged in life, and are determined. Do not discuss your love life. If the story you tell is about your professional life, make sure it shows you working productively as a member of a team on some worthwhile project that had problems but which came out okay in the end. Alternatively, tell stories that in some way show you employing *transferable skills* and *professional values* in some subtle way.

What have you learned from jobs you have held?

You've learned that little gets achieved without *teamwork*, and that there's invariably sound thinking behind *systems and procedures*. To get to the root of problems it's better to talk less and listen more. Most of all, you've learned that you can either sit on the sidelines watching the hours go by or you can get involved and make a difference with your presence. You do the latter because you're goal-oriented, time goes quicker when you're engaged, and besides, the relationships you build are with better people. You might finish with: "There are two general things I have learned from past jobs. First, if you are confused, ask— it's better to ask a dumb question than make a dumb mistake. Second, it's better to promise less and produce more than to make unrealistic forecasts."

Define "cooperation."

The question examines *manageability* and asks you to explain how you see your responsibilities as a *team player*, both in taking direction and working for the overall success of your department. Your answer will define "cooperation" as doing your job in a way that enables your colleagues to do theirs with a minimum of disruption. It's your desire to be part of something significant: Through hard work and good will, to make the team something greater than the sum of its parts.

What difficulties do you have tolerating people with backgrounds and interests different from yours?

Another "team player" question with the awkward implication that you do have problems. Say, "I don't have any." But don't leave it there.

"I don't have any problems working with people from different backgrounds. In fact, I find it energizing; with different backgrounds, you get different life experiences and different ways of coming at problems. The opportunity to work with people different from yourself is golden."

In hindsight, what have you done that was a little harebrained?

You are never harebrained in your business dealings, and you haven't been harebrained in your personal life since graduation, right? The only safe examples to use are ones from your deep past that ultimately turned out well. One of the best, if it applies to you, is: "Well, I guess the time I bought my house. I had no idea what I was letting myself in for and didn't pay enough attention to how much work the place would need. Still, there weren't any big structural problems, though I had to put a lot of work into fixing it up the way I wanted. Yes, my first house—that was a real learning experience." Not only can most people relate to this example, but it also gives you the opportunity to sell one or two of your very positive and endearing professional behaviors.

You've been given a project that requires you to interact with different levels of the company. How do you do this? What levels are you most comfortable with?

This is a two-part question that probes communication and self-confidence skills. The first part asks how you interact with superiors and motivate those working with and for you on the project. The second part is saying, "Tell me whom you regard as your peer group—help me categorize you." To cover those bases, include the essence of this: "There are two types of people I would interact with on a project of this nature. First, there are those I would report to, who would bear the ultimate responsibility for the project's success. With them, I would determine deadlines and a method for evaluating the success of the project. I would outline my approach, breaking the project down into component parts, getting approval on both the approach and the costs. I would keep my supervisors updated on a regular basis and seek input whenever needed. My supervisors would expect three things from me: the facts, an analysis of potential problems, and that I not be intimidated, as this would jeopardize the project's success. I would comfortably satisfy those expectations.

"The other people to interact with on a project like this are those who work with and for me. With those people, I would outline the project and explain how a successful outcome will benefit the company. I would assign the component parts to those best suited to each, and arrange follow-up times to assure completion by deadline. My role here would be to facilitate, motivate, and bring the different personalities together to form a team.

"As for comfort level, I find this type of approach enables me to interact comfortably with all levels and types of people."

Tell me about an event that really challenged you. How did you meet the challenge? In what way was your approach different from that of others?

This is a straightforward, two-part question. The first part probes your *critical thinking skills*. The second asks you to set yourself apart from the herd. Outline the root of the problem, its significance, and its negative impact on the department/company. The clearer you make the situation, the better. Having done so, explain your solution, its value to your employer, and how it was different from other approaches:

"My company has offices all around the country; I am responsible for seventy of them. My job is to visit each office on a regular basis and build market-penetration strategies with management, and to train and motivate the sales and customer service forces. When the recession hit, the need to service those offices was greater than ever, yet the traveling costs were getting prohibitive.

"Morale was an especially important factor: You can't let outlying offices feel defeated. I reapportioned my budget and did the following: I dramatically increased telephone contact with the offices and instituted weekly sales-technique e-mails and monthly training webinars—how to prospect for new clients, how to negotiate difficult sales, and so forth. I increased management training, again using webinars and concentrating on how to run sales meetings, early termination of low producers, and so forth.

"While my colleagues complained about the drop in sales, mine increased, albeit by a modest 6 percent. After two quarters, the new media/coaching approach was officially adopted by the company."

> Give me an example of a method of working you have used. How did you feel about it?

You have a choice of giving an example of either good or bad work habits. Give a good example, one that demonstrates your understanding of corporate goals and your organizational or *critical thinking skills*. If you have taken the time to develop the time-management and organization skills that underlie *multitasking* abilities, you have a great illustrative example to use.

You could say: "Maximum productivity requires focus and demands organization and time management. I do my paperwork at the end of each day, when I review the day's achievements; with this done, I plan for tomorrow, prioritizing all projected activities. When I come to work in the morning, I'm ready to get going without wasting time and sure that I will be spending my time and effort in the areas where it is most needed to deliver results. I try to schedule meetings right before lunch; people get to the point more quickly if it's on their time. I feel this is an efficient and organized method of working."

In working with new people, how do you go about getting an understanding of them?

Every new hire is expected to become a viable part of the group, which means getting an understanding of the group and its individual members. Understanding that everyone likes to give advice is the key to your answer. You have found that the best way to understand and become part of a new team is to be open, friendly, ask lots of questions, and be helpful whenever you can. The answers to your questions give you needed insights into the ways of the job, department, and company, and they help you get to know the person.

What would your references say about you?

You have nothing to lose by giving a positive answer. If you checked your references, as I recommended earlier, you can give details of what your best references will say. When you demonstrate how well you and your boss got along, the interviewer does not have to ask, "What do you dislike about your current manager?"

Every interview is a stress interview, but sometimes interviewers will ratchet up the stress level. You need to be ready, and that's where we're headed next.

CHAPTER 11

HOW TO HANDLE STRESS AND ILLEGAL QUESTIONS

THERE IS NO GREATER FEAR THAN FEAR OF THE UNKNOWN, and that is exactly what you worry about going into a job interview; this worry increases your anxiety level.

While interviewers categorically deny conducting stress interviews, they readily admit that if there is stress on the job, they need to know how a candidate will react to it. Often they will try to recreate it by throwing in the occasional question to see how a candidate maintains her balance: Does she remain calm and analytical? Does her mind still process effectively when under pressure? Can she express herself effectively, and is she in control while managing stressful situations?

Any question you are unprepared for can cause stress. Interviewers can create stress unintentionally, or can consciously use stress to simulate the unexpected and sometimes tense events of everyday business life. Seeing how you handle the unexpected in a job interview gives a fair indication of how you will react to the unexpected when it crops up in real life.

Interviewers are looking for the candidate who stays calm and continues to process incoming information during stressful events and, having processed it, asks questions for clarification or responds professionally with appropriate actions and/or words.

If you are ill-prepared for an interview, no one will be able to put more pressure on you than you do on yourself. The only way to combat the stress you feel from fear of the unknown is to be prepared, to know what the stress questions might be and what the interviewer is trying to discover with them, and to prepare your strategies for these situations. Remember: A stress interview is just a regular interview with the volume turned all the way up—the music is the same, just louder.

How do you go about solving problems in your work?

Every position, from CEO to fast-food server, has its problems and challenges. This question examines your *critical thinking skills*, and asks you to explain your approach to problem solving. There is an established approach to problem solving that everyone who gets ahead in his professional life learns: When confronted with a problem, take these steps:

- Define the problem.
- Identify why it's a problem and whom it's a problem for.
- Identify what's causing the problem.
- Seek input from everyone affected by the problem.
- Identify possible solutions.
- Identify the time, cost, and resources it will take to implement each option.
- Evaluate the consequences of each solution.
- Decide upon the best solution.
- Identify and execute the steps necessary to solve the problem.

Your answer should cover these steps. If asked for a real-world example, you'll have plenty in mind from your TJD exercises. Remember to recall the results and benefits of your solution and the *transferable skills* that came into play.

With hindsight, how could you have improved your progress?

This is a question that asks you to discuss your commitment to success. As professional success affects so many other parts of your life, take time to think through the mistakes you have made and commit to getting better control of your career for the future. Whatever you choose to say, when it comes to questions asking for information detrimental to your candidacy, always put your answer in the past: You woke up, took responsibility, and corrected the situation. Show that, having learned from the experience, you are now committed to ongoing professional development.

What kinds of decisions are most difficult for you?

You are human—admit it, but be careful what you admit. The employer is looking for people who can make decisions and solve problems, not those who'll dither instead of do. You want to come off as someone who's decisive but not precipitate, who considers the implications of actions on outcomes, any side effects those actions might have on other activities, and whether they conflict with existing *systems and procedures* or other company priorities.

If you have ever had to fire someone, you are in luck, because no one likes to do that. Emphasize that, having reached a logical conclusion, you act. If you are not in management, tie your answer to *transferable skills* and *professional values*: "It's not that I have difficulty making decisions—some just require more consideration than others. A small example might be vacation time. Now, everyone is entitled to it, but I don't believe you should leave your boss in a bind. I think very carefully at the beginning of the year when I'd like to take my vacation, and then think of alternate dates. I go to my supervisor, tell him what I hope to do, and see whether there is any conflict. I wouldn't want to be out of the office for the two weeks prior to a project deadline, for instance. So by carefully considering things far enough in advance, I make sure my plans jibe with my boss and the department for the year."

Here you take a trick question and use it to demonstrate your consideration, analytical abilities, and concern for the department—and for the company's bottom line.

Tell me about the problems you have living within your means.

If you have experienced severe financial difficulties, you'll need to address them and how they have been handled. Think through your answer carefully and keep it short, emphasizing that you are in control of the situation. Otherwise, say that you continually strive to improve your skills and your living standard: "I know few people who are satisfied with their current earnings. As a professional, I am continually striving to improve my skills and my living standard. But my problems are no different from those of this or any other company—making sure all the bills get paid on time and recognizing that every month and year there are some things that are prudent to do and others that are best deferred."

What area of your skills/professional development do you want to improve at this time?

Another "tell me all your weaknesses" question. Don't damage your candidacy with careless admissions of weakness. Choose a skill where you are competent but that everyone, including the interviewer, knows demands constant personal attention. *Technology skills* as they apply to your job could be a good example of a "weakness" that every committed professional shares. Cite the importance and challenge of staying current in this area and finish with saying, "_____is so important, I don't think I will ever stop paying attention to this area." Be prepared to explain how you are working on this skill development right now. "In fact, I'm reading a book on this now," or "I'm taking another course next . . ." There are plenty of books and online courses on every topic under the sun, so if you are engaged in your career, you should be able to give some details.

One effective answer to this is to say, "Well, from what you told me about the job, I seem to have all the necessary skills and background. What I would really find exciting is the opportunity to work on a job where . . ." At this point, you replay the skill-development area you cited. This approach allows you to emphasize what you find exciting about the job and that you have all the required *technical skills* and are proactively committed to professional skill development. It works admirably.

You can finish with saying, "These areas are so important that I don't think anyone can be too good or should ever stop trying to polish their skills."

> *Your application shows you have been with one company a long time without any appreciable increase in rank or salary. Tell me about this.*

Analyze why this state of affairs exists. It may be that you like your professional life exactly as it is. You take *pride* in your work and haven't pushed for promotions. If so, tell it like it is, because most people are eager for a promotion—someone who isn't could make for a good hire; it could be your ace.

Here are some tactics you can use. First of all, try to avoid putting your salary history on application forms. No one is going to deny you an interview for lack of a salary history if your skills match those the job requires. And of course, you should never put such unnecessary information on your resume.

Now, we'll address the delicate matter of "Hey, wait a minute; why no promotions?" The interviewer has posed a truly negative inquiry. The more time either of you spend on it, the more time the interviewer gets to devote to concentrating on negative aspects of your candidacy. Make your answer short and sweet, then shut up. For instance, "My current employer is a stable company with a good working environment, but there's minimal growth there in my area—in fact, there hasn't been any promotion in my area since _____ . Your question is the reason I am meeting here with you; I have the skills and ability to take on more responsibility, and I'm looking for a place to do that."

> *In your current job, what should you spend more time on and why?*

Without a little self-control you could easily blurt out what you consider to be your greatest weaknesses. Tricky question, but with a little forethought your answer will shine.

Enlightened self-interest dictates that your ongoing career-management strategies identify and develop the skills demanded in a constantly changing work environment that make you desirable to employers, and that each of your job changes should occur within the context of an overall career management strategy.

So your answer might address the fact that existing skills always need to be improved and new skills acquired, citing an example of some skill development initiative you are working on now. Unless you are in sales/marketing, you could add that with networking seen as so important by everyone today, you should probably be investing more time in that; in sales and marketing, of course, this is your very lifeblood.

Your answer might include, "With the fast pace of change in our profession, existing skills always need to be improved and new skills learned. For instance, in this job I think the organizational software now available can have a major impact on personal productivity. If I stayed with my current employer this would be a priority, just as it will be when I make the move to my next job; it's in my own best interests to have good skills." With an answer along these lines you show foresight instead of a weakness. You can then end with:

- Courses you have taken and are planning to take
- Books you have read or book clubs you belong to
- Memberships in professional associations
- Subscriptions to professional journals

Such an answer will identify you as an aware, connected, and dedicated professional.

Are you willing to take calculated risks when necessary?

Confirm your understanding of the question by qualifying it: "How do you define calculated risks? Can you give me an example?" or "Would you run that by me again?" This will give you more information as well as more time to think while the interviewer repeats the question in more detail. (You can use this "qualifying the question" technique with tough questions when you want a little recovery time.)

Once you understand the question, you'll probably answer, "Yes," if you want the job offer. Be prepared with an example for the possible follow-up question showing how your calculations and preparation minimize potential risk. Whatever your answer, the risk taken must be within the normal bounds of the execution of your duties and in no way jeopardize colleagues or company.

See this pen I'm holding? Sell it to me.

This question often comes up for sales professionals, but every employee needs to know how to *communicate* effectively and sell appropriately—sometimes products, but more often ideas, approaches, and concepts. This is what the interviewer is getting at with this apparently out-of-the-blue request.

As such, you are being examined about your understanding of constitutive/needs-based/features and benefits sales, how quickly you think on your feet, and how effectively you use verbal communication. For example, say the interviewer holds up a yellow highlighter. First, you will want to establish the customer's needs with a few questions like, "What sort of pens do you currently use? Do you use a highlighter? Do you read reports and need to recall important points? Is comfort important to you?" Then you will proceed calmly, "Let me tell you about the special features of this pen and show you how it will satisfy your needs. First of all, it is tailor-made for highlighting reports, and that will save you time in recalling the most important points. The case is wide for comfort and the base is flat so it will stand up and be visible on a cluttered work area. It's disposable—and affordable enough to have a handful for desk, briefcase, car, and home. And the bright yellow means you'll never lose it." Then close with a smile and a question of your own that will bring a smile to the interviewer's face: "How many gross shall we deliver?"

How will you be able to cope with a change in environment after _____ years with your current company?

Another chance to take an implied negative and turn it into a positive: "That's one of the reasons I want to make a change. After five years with my current employer, I felt I was about to get stale. I have exemplary skills in _____, _____, and _____. It's just time for me to take these skills to a new and more challenging environment and experience some new thinking and approaches. Hopefully, I'll have the chance to contribute with my experience."

Why aren't you earning more at your age?

Accept this as a compliment to your skills and accomplishments. "I have always felt that solid experience would put me in good stead in the long run and that earnings would come in due course. Also, I am not the type of person to change jobs just for the money. At this point, I have a set of desirable skills [*itemize them as they relate to the job's priorities*] and the time has come for me to join a team that needs and values these skills. How much *should* I be earning now?" The figure could be your offer.

What is the worst thing you have heard about our company?

This question can come as something of a shock. As with all stress questions, your poise under stress is vital: If you can carry off a halfway decent answer as well, you are a winner. The best response to this question is simple. Just say with a smile and a laugh: "You are a tough company to get an interview with, and you demand a lot of your employees. But I actually like that about you, because I'm looking to gain the sort of expertise that will facilitate my professional growth." This way you compliment the company and pass off the negative judgment as a misperception by all those *other* jerks who think hard work is a bad thing.

Why should I hire an outsider when I could fill the job with someone inside the company?

The question isn't as stupid as it sounds. Obviously, the interviewer has examined existing employees with an eye toward their promotion or reassignment. Just as obviously, the job cannot be filled from within the company. If it could be, it would be, and for two very good reasons: It is cheaper for the company to promote from within, and it is better for employee morale.

Hiding behind this intimidating question is a pleasant invitation: "Tell me why I should hire you." Your answer should include two steps. The first is a recitation of your *technical* and *transferable skills*, tailored to the job's needs.

For the second step, realize first that whenever a manager is filling a position, she is looking not only for someone who can do the job, but also for someone who can benefit the department in a larger sense. No department is as good as it could be—each has weaknesses that need strengthening. So in the second part of your answer, include a question of your own: "Those are my general attributes. However, if no one is promotable from inside the company, you must be looking to add strength to your team in a special way. How do you hope the final candidate will be able to benefit your department?" The answer to this is your cue to sell your applicable qualities.

Have you ever had any financial difficulties?

A common question, especially if you deal with money. Tell the truth because when references are checked, salary and credit are at the top of the list. Your answer succinctly gives the circumstances, the facts of your difficulties, and where you stand today in resolving those issues. Do not bring up financial problems until this question is asked or an offer is on the table and references are to be checked.

For someone to check your credit history, he must have your written consent. This is required under the 1972 Fair Credit and Reporting Act. Invariably, when you fill out a job application form, sign it, and date it, you've also signed a release permitting the employer to check your credit history.

If you have had to file for bankruptcy, it will show up in a credit check, so be honest, professional, and as brief as possible. Don't give any information about the circumstances: It isn't necessary and no one wants to know. What an employer does want to hear is that you have turned the corner and everything is under control now. She also wants to know, very briefly, what you learned and have done to rebuild your credit and get back on your feet.

Financial difficulties aren't the deal-breaker they used to be, unless they affect the employer's insurance obligations, and in light of the corporate and personal financial crises of recent years, many corporations are re-evaluating and taking a more realistic stance on these matters. Once it's behind you, get it expunged from your record.

How should I handle a DWI?

Find out if it will show up on a background check, as procedures differ from state to state. If the application asks, answer and leave it be; if not, don't offer this information until background checks are close. Then be brief—"It happened, I was young, etc."—and stress what you learned from it. Try to get it expunged: Google "DWI expunge."

How should I handle a felony?

First, determine if it's on your record, if it will show up in a background check, and what employers in your state can take into consideration. States handle felony records differently, as they do the information an employer may inquire about. Learn what you have to disclose to an employer and don't disclose more than you have to. Briefly, tell the employer what you've learned and that it is behind you. Discrepancies between your application and convictions can cause problems.

There's no need to discuss issues that didn't result in conviction or anything that has been expunged.

Tell me about a time things didn't work out well.

There are two techniques that every skilled interviewer will use, especially if you are giving good answers. In this question, the interviewer looks for negative balance; in the follow-up, the person will look for negative confirmation. Here, you are required to give an example of an inadequacy. The trick is to pull something from the past, not the present, and to finish with what you learned from the experience. For example: "That's easy. When I first joined the workforce, I didn't really understand the importance of systems and procedures. There was this sales visit report everyone had to fill out after visiting a customer. I always put a lot of effort into it, until I realized it was never read; it just went in a file. So I stopped doing it for a few days to see if it made any difference. I thought I was gaining time to make more sales for the company. I was so proud of my extra sales calls, I told my boss at the end of the week. My boss explained that the records were for the long term, so that should my job change, the next salesperson would have the benefit of a full client history. It was a long time ago, but I have never forgotten the lesson: There's always a reason for systems and procedures. I've had the best-kept records in the company ever since."

To look for negative confirmation, the interviewer may then say something like, "Thank you. Now can you give me another example?" He is trying to confirm a weakness. If you help, you could cost yourself the job. Here's your reaction: You sit deep in thought for a good ten seconds, then look up and say firmly, "No, that's the only occasion when anything like that happened." Shut up and refuse to be enticed further.

Tell me about a time when you put your foot in your mouth.

Answer this question with caution. The interviewer is examining your ability and willingness to interact pleasantly with others. The question is tricky because it asks you to show yourself in a poor light. Downplay the negative impact of your action and end with positive information about your candidacy. The best thing to do is to start with an example outside of the workplace and show how the experience improved your performance at work.

"About five years ago, I let the cat out of the bag about a surprise birthday party for a friend, a terrific faux pas. It was a mortifying experience, and I promised myself not to let anything like that happen again." Then, after this fairly innocuous statement, you can talk about communications in the workplace: "As far as work is concerned, I always regard employer-employee communications on any matter as confidential unless expressly stated otherwise. So, putting my foot in my mouth doesn't happen to me at work."

What was there about your last company that you didn't particularly like or agree with?

Be careful not to criticize a manager, or you might be seen as a potential management problem. It is safest to say that you didn't have any of these problems. If there was an unhappy work environment and this opinion was shared by many, you can mention it, but remain nonspecific, although you might say that some people didn't seem to care about anything they did, and you found this difficult.

Another option: "I didn't like the way some people gave lip service to the 'customer comes first' mantra, but really didn't go out of their way to keep the customer satisfied. I don't think it was a fault of management, just a general malaise that seemed to affect a lot of people."

What do you feel is a satisfactory attendance record?

There are two answers to this question—one if you are in management, and one if you are not. As a manager: "I believe attendance is a matter of management, motivation, and psychology. Letting the employees know you expect their best efforts and won't accept half-baked excuses is one part. The other is to keep your employees motivated by a congenial work environment and the challenge to stretch themselves. Giving people pride in their work and letting them know you respect them as individuals have a lot to do with it, too."

If you are not in management, the answer is even easier: "I've never really considered it. I work for a living, I enjoy my job, and I'm rarely sick."

What is your general impression of your last company?

Always answer positively. There is a strong belief in management ranks that people who complain about past employers will cause problems for their new ones. Your answer is, "A good department and company to work for." Then smile and wait for the next question. If pressed for more, add, "I had gone as far as I could and could see no opportunities opening up, so I determined it was time to make a strategic career move."

What are some of the things you find difficult to do? Why do you feel that way?

Your answer should share a difficulty common to the job and everyone who does it.

"That's a tough question. There are so many things that are difficult to stay current with, considering the pace of business today and pace of change that technology brings to our profession. One of my problems has been staying on top of the customer base in a productive and responsible fashion. I built my territory and had 140 clients to sell to every month, and I was so busy touching base with all of them that I never got a chance to sell to any of them. So I graded them into three groups. I called on the top 20 percent of my clients every three weeks. The balance of my clients I called on once a month, but with a difference—each month, I marked ten of them to spend time with and really get to know. I still have difficulty reaching all my clients in a month, but with time management, prioritization, and organization, my sales have tripled and are still climbing."

Jobs have pluses and minuses. What were some of the minuses on your last job?

A variation on the question, "What interests you least about this job?" which was handled earlier. Potentially explosive but easily defused. Regardless of your occupation, there is at least one repetitive, mindless duty that everyone groans about but which has to be done. You just need to show that you recognize its importance despite the boredom factor and take care of business responsibly. For example, "Client visit reports are probably the least exciting part of my job. However, I know they are important for reference and continuity, so I do them at the end of the day as part of my daily performance review and next-day planning." This response answers the question without shooting yourself in the foot, and shows that you possess *critical thinking* and *multitasking skills*. You can finish with a nod toward your *professional values* and *teamwork skills*. "Besides, if I don't do the paperwork, that holds up other people in the company."

Or perhaps, "In accounts receivable, it's my job to get the money in to make payroll and good things like that. Half the time, the goods get shipped before I get the paperwork because sales says, 'It's a rush order.' That's a real minus to me. It was so bad at my last company that we tried a new approach. We met with sales and explained our problem. The result was that incremental commissions were based on cash in, not on bill date. They saw the connection, and things are much better now."

What kinds of people do you like to work with?

This is the easy part of what can be a tricky three-part question. Obviously, you like to work with people who are fully engaged in their work and who come to work with a smile and want to make a difference with their presence; with people who are there to get results, not just mark time till the end of the day. You like to work with people who have *pride*, honesty, *integrity*, and *commitment* to their work.

What kinds of people do you find it difficult to work with?

This question can stand alone or can be the second part of a three-part question. Your answer comes from understanding why your job exists: It's a small cog in the complex machinery that makes a company profitable, so you might say, "People who don't care about their work and don't care about being part of something larger than themselves, people who have the time to find fault but not to find solutions." End by noting that while they aren't the best coworkers, you don't let them interfere with your *motivation*.

Or, "People who don't follow procedures, or slackers—the occasional rotten apples who don't really care about the quality of their work. They're long on complaints, but short on solutions."

How have you successfully worked with this difficult type of person?

Sometimes this question stands alone; other times it's the third part of a three-part question. First, you don't let such people affect your *motivation* or quality of work. Second, you don't buy into their negativism by encouraging them. You are polite and professional, but prefer to ally yourself with the people who come to work to make a difference. You maintain cordial relations, but don't go out of your way to seek close acquaintance. Life is too short to be demotivated by people who think their cup is half empty and it's someone else's fault.

Or you might reply with something like: "I stick to my guns, stay enthusiastic, and hope some of it will rub off. I had a big problem with one guy—all he did was complain, and always in my area. Eventually, I told him how I felt. I said if I were a millionaire, I'd clearly have all the answers and wouldn't have to work, but as it was, I wasn't, and had to work for a living. I told him that I really enjoyed his company but I didn't want to hear it anymore. Every time I saw him after that, I presented him with a work problem and asked his advice. In other words I challenged him to come up with positives, not negatives."

You might even end by noting that sometimes you've noticed that such people simply lack enthusiasm and confidence, and that energetic and cheerful coworkers can often change that.

How did you get your last job?

The interviewer is looking for initiative. Show that you went about your search with planning, *organization*, and intelligence, the same way you'd approach a work project. At least show *determination*. For example: "I was turned down for my last job for having too little experience. I asked the manager to give me a trial for the afternoon, then and there. I was given a list of companies they'd never sold to. I picked up the phone and didn't get close to a sale all afternoon, but she could see I had guts."

How would you evaluate me as an interviewer?

The question is dangerous, maybe more so than the one asking you to criticize your boss. If you think the interviewer is a congenital imbecile whom you wouldn't work for on a bet, don't tell the truth, because behind this question is a desire to see your verbal and diplomacy skills in action. This is one instance where honesty is *not* the best policy: Remember, you are there to get a job offer. It is best to say, "This is one of the toughest interviews I have ever been through, and I don't relish the prospect of going through another. I have great professional skills, but interviewing is not one of them; it's not something I have had much experience doing. Yet I do realize that you are just trying to determine if I have the skills you need." Then go on to explain how your skills match the job. You may choose to finish the answer with a question of your own: "I think I can do this job, and I think I would like it. What do you think?"

Wouldn't you feel better off in another company?

Relax, things aren't as bad as you might assume. This question is usually asked if you are really doing quite well or if the job involves a certain amount of stress. A lawyer, for example, might well be expected to face this one. The trick is not to be intimidated. Your first step is to qualify the question. Relax, take a breath, sit back, smile, and say, "You surprise me. Why do you say that?" The interviewer must then talk, giving you precious time to collect your wits and come back with a rebuttal.

Then answer "no," and explain why. All the interviewer wants to see is how much you know about the company and how determined you are to join its ranks. Overcome the objection with an example showing how you will contribute to the company. You could reply: "Not at all. My whole experience has been with small companies. I am good at my job and in time could become a big fish in a little pond. But that is not what I want. This corporation is a leader in its business. You have a strong reputation for encouraging skills development in your employees. This is the type of environment I want to work in. Coming from a small company, I have done a little bit of everything. That means that no matter what you throw at me, I will learn it quickly."

Then end with a question of your own. In this instance, the question has a twofold purpose: first, to identify a critical area to sell yourself; and second, to encourage the interviewer to imagine you working at the company: "For example, what will be the first project you'll need me to tackle?"

You end with a question of your own that gets the interviewer focusing on those immediate problems. You can then move the conversation forward with an explanation of how your background and experience can help.

> *What would you say if I told you that your presentation this afternoon was lousy?*

This question is asked to help a manager understand how emotionally mature you are. When it is a manager's duty to criticize performance, she needs to know that you will respond in a professional and *emotionally mature* way.

"If" is the key word in the question. The question tests your poise, *critical thinking*, and *communication skills*. Don't assume you are being criticized. An appropriate response would be: "First of all, I would ask which aspects of my presentation were lousy. I would need to find out where you felt the problem was. If there were miscommunication, I'd clear it up. If the problem were elsewhere, I would seek your advice, confirm that I understood it, and be sure that the problem did not recur."

Building Stress Into a Sequence of Questions

Sometimes an interviewer will build stress into a sequence of questions. Starting off innocently enough, the questions are layered and sequenced to dig deeper and deeper, but these stress question sequences will hold few surprises for you. Let's take the simple example of "Can you work under pressure?"

This example will use a reporter's technique of asking who, what, where, when, why, and how. The technique can be applied to any question you are asked and is frequently used to probe those success stories that sound too good to be true. You'll find them suddenly tagged on to the simple closed-ended questions as well as to the open-ended ones. They can often start with phrases like: "Share with me," "Tell me about a time when," or "I'm interested in finding out about," followed by a request for specific examples from your work history.

> Can you work under pressure?

A simple, closed-ended question that requires just a yes-or-no answer, but you won't get off so easy.

> Good, I'd be interested to hear about a time when you experienced pressure on your job.

An open-ended request to tell a story about a pressure situation. After this, you will be subjected to the layering technique—six layers in the following instance.

> Why do you think this situation arose?

It's best if the situation you describe is not a peer's or manager's fault. Remember, you must be seen as a team player.

> How do you feel others involved could have acted more responsibly?

An open invitation to criticize peers and superiors, which you should diplomatically decline.

Who holds the responsibility for the situation?

Another invitation to point the finger of blame, which should be avoided.

Where in the chain of command could steps be taken to avoid that sort of thing happening again?

This question probes your analytical skills and asks whether you are the type of person who takes the time to revisit the scene of the crime to learn for the next time.

After you've survived that barrage, a friendly tone may conceal another zinger: "What did you learn from the experience?" This question is geared to probe your judgment and *emotional maturity*. Your answer should emphasize whichever of the key professional behaviors your story was illustrating.

When an interviewer feels you were on the edge of revealing something unusual in an answer, you may well encounter "mirror statements." Here, the last key phrase of your answer will be repeated or paraphrased, and followed by a steady gaze and silence. For example, "So, you learned that organization is the key to management." The idea is that the silence and an expectant look will work together to keep you talking. It can be disconcerting to find yourself rambling on without quite knowing why. The trick is knowing when to stop. When the interviewer gives you an expectant look in this context, expand your answer (you have to), but by no more than a couple of sentences. Otherwise, you will get that creepy feeling that you're digging yourself into a hole.

The Illegal Question

Of course, one of the most stressful—and negative—questions is the illegal one, a question that delves into your private life or personal background. Such a question will make you uncomfortable if it is blatant, and could also make you angry.

Your aim, however, is to overcome your discomfort and avoid getting angry: You want to get the job offer, and any self-righteous or defensive reaction on your part will ensure that you don't. You may feel angry enough to get up and walk out, or say things like, "These are unfair practices; you'll hear from my lawyer in the morning." But the result will be that you won't get the offer, and therefore won't have the leverage you need. Remember, no one is saying you can't refuse the job once it's offered to you.

So what is an illegal question? Title VII of the Civil Rights Act of 1964 is a federal law that forbids employers from discriminating against any person on the basis of sex, age, race, national origin, or religion. More recently, the Americans with Disabilities Act was passed to protect this important minority.

- **An interviewer may not ask** about your religion, church, synagogue, or parish, the religious holidays you observe, or your political beliefs or affiliations. He may not ask, for instance, "Does your religion allow you to work on Saturdays?" But he *may* ask something like, "This job requires work on Saturdays. Is that a problem?"

- **An interviewer may not ask** about your ancestry, national origin, or parentage; in addition, you cannot be asked about the naturalization status of your parents, spouse, or children. The interviewer cannot ask about your birthplace. But she may ask (and probably will, considering the current immigration laws) whether you are a U.S. citizen or a resident alien with the right to work in the United States.

- **An interviewer may not ask** about your native language, the language you speak at home, or how you acquired the ability to read, write, or speak a foreign language. But he may ask about the languages in which you are fluent if knowledge of those languages is pertinent to the job.

- **An interviewer may not ask** about your age, your date of birth, whether you are married or pregnant, or the ages of your children. But she may ask you whether you are over eighteen years old.

- **An interviewer may not ask** about maiden names or whether you have changed your name; your marital status, number of children or dependents, or your spouse's occupation; or whether (if you are a woman) you wish to be addressed as Miss, Mrs., or Ms. But the interviewer may ask about how you like to be addressed (a common courtesy) and whether you have ever worked for the company before under a different name. (If you have worked for this company or other companies under a different name, you may want to mention that, in light of the fact that this prospective manager may check your references and additional background information.)

As you consider a question that seems to verge on illegality, take into account that the interviewer may be asking it innocently and may be unaware of the laws on the matter. Even more likely is that the interviewer really likes you, and is interested in you as a person. When we meet someone new, often some of the first questions will be: Where are you from? Are you married? Have kids? What church do you go to? Bear this in mind so that you don't overreact.

Your best bet is to be polite and straightforward, just as you would be in any other social situation. You also want to move the conversation to an examination of your skills and abilities, and away from personal issues. Here are some common illegal questions—and possible responses. Remember as you frame your answers to the occasional illegal question that your objective is to get job offers; if you later decide that this company is not for you, you are under no obligation to accept the position.

What religion do you practice?

In most instances, an interviewer may not ask about religious beliefs. However, as with most illegal questions, it's sometimes in your interest to answer.

You might say, "I attend my church/synagogue/mosque regularly, but I make it my practice not to involve my personal beliefs in my work." Or, "I have a set of beliefs that are important to me, but I do not mix those beliefs with my work, and understand this is something employers don't want their people discussing."

If you do not practice a religion, you may want to say something like, "I have a set of personal beliefs that are important to me, but I do not attend organized services at present. And I do not mix those beliefs with my work, if that's what you mean."

Are you married?

If you are, the company is concerned about the impact your family duties and future plans will have on your tenure there. Although illegal if it is asked, it's best to answer this question and remove any doubts the interviewer might otherwise have. Your answer could be, "Yes, I am. Of course, I make a separation between my work life and my family life that allows me to give my all to a job. I have no problem with travel or late hours; those things are part of my work and family obligations have never interfered. My references will confirm this for you."

Do you have/plan to have children?

Most often asked of women in their childbearing years. This isn't any of the interviewer's business, but she may be concerned about whether you will leave the company early to raise a family. Behind the question is the impact of absences on departmental deliverables. You could always answer "no." If you answer "yes," you might qualify it, "but those plans are for way in the future, and they depend on the success of my career. Certainly, I want to do the best, most complete job I can for this company. I consider that my skills are right for the job and that I can make a long-term contribution. I certainly have no plans to leave the company just as I begin to make meaningful contributions."

If the questions become too pointed, you may want to ask—innocently—"Could you explain the relevance of that issue to the position?" That response, however, can seem confrontational; you should only use it if you are extremely uncomfortable or are quite certain you can get away with it. Sometimes, the interviewer will drop the line of questioning.

Illegal questions tend to arise not out of brazen insensitivity but rather out of an interest in you. The employer is familiar with your skills and background, feels you can do the job, and wants to get to know you as a person. Outright discrimination these days is really quite rare. With illegal questions, your response must be positive—that's the only way you're going to get the job offer.

CHAPTER 12

WELCOME TO THE REAL WORLD

AS A RECENT GRADUATE, MOST LIKELY ENTERING THE PROFESSIONAL WORLD for the first time, you can expect questions designed to determine your potential.

Corporate recruiters liken the gamble of hiring recent graduates to laying down wines for the future: Some will develop into full-bodied, excellent vintages, but others will be disappointments. When hiring professionals with work experience, there is a track record to evaluate; with recent graduates, there is little or nothing. Often, the only solid things an interviewer has to go on are the degree, SAT scores, and that ubiquitous burger-flipping job. That's not much on which to base a hiring decision.

Of all the steps you will take up the ladder of success over the years, none is more important or more difficult than getting a foot on that first rung. You have no idea how the professional game is played and you are up against thousands of other recent grads with pretty much the same to offer. Differentiating yourself by demonstrating your understanding of the professional world and your motivation and potential will be important tools in helping get your career off to a good start.

Interviewers will be especially interested in what you have done to show initiative, and how willing you are to learn, grow, and get the job done.

Your goal is to stand out from all the other entry-level candidates as someone altogether different: You are more engaged in the success of your professional life, more knowledgeable about the job and the world in which it functions, and more prepared to listen, learn, and do whatever it takes to earn your place on a professional team. Don't be like thousands of others who, in answer to questions about their greatest strength, reply lamely, "I'm good with people," or, "I like working with others." Answers like this brand you as average. To stand out, a recent graduate must recount a past situation that illustrates *how* she is good with people, or one that demonstrates an ability to be a team player.

Fortunately, the *transferable skills* and *professional values* discussed throughout the book are just as helpful for getting your foot on the ladder as they are for increasing your employability and aiding your climb to the top.

It isn't necessary to have snap answers ready for every question, and you never will. It is more important for you to pause after a question and collect your thoughts before answering. That pause shows that you think before you speak, an admired trait in the professional world. Remember that *critical thinking* is one of the *transferable skills*.

Asking for a question to be repeated is useful to gain time and is quite acceptable, as long as you don't do it with every question. And if a question stumps you, as sometimes happens, do not stutter incoherently. It is sometimes best to say, "I don't know" or, "I'd like to come back to that later." Odds are the interviewer will forget to ask again; if he does come back to it, at least your mind, processing in the background, has had some time to come up with an answer.

The following questions are commonly asked of entry-level professionals, but these are not the only questions you will be asked, so you will still need to study the other chapters on turning interviews into offers. For example, the first two questions you are likely to face at almost every job interview you go to over your entire career are: "Tell me a little about yourself" and "What do you know about our company?" The questions in this chapter are just those aimed exclusively at entry-level professionals.

How did you get your summer jobs?

Employers look favorably on recent graduates who have any work experience, no matter what it is. "It is far easier to get a fix on someone who has worked while at school," says Dan O'Brien, head of employment at Grumman. "They manage their time better, are more realistic, and more mature. Any work experience gives us much more in common." So, as you think about some of those crummy jobs you held, take the time to think, in hindsight, about what you actually learned about the professional world from that experience. At the very least, you learned that business is about making a profit, doing things more efficiently, adhering to *systems and procedures* (which are always there for good reason), and putting in whatever effort it takes to get the job done. In short, treat your summer jobs, no matter how humble, as a launch pad for greater things. It has been wisely said that it's not the job that defines you; it's what you bring to the job.

In this particular question, the interviewer is looking for something that shows initiative, creativity, and flexibility. Here's an example: "In my town, summer jobs were hard to come by, but I applied to each local restaurant for a position waiting tables, called the manager at each one to arrange an interview, and finally landed a job at one of the most prestigious. I was assigned to the afternoon shift, but because of my quick work, accurate billing, and ability to keep customers happy, they soon moved me to the evening shift. I worked there for three summers, and by the time I left, I was responsible for the training and management of the night-shift waiters, the allotment of tips, and the evening's final closing and accounting. All in all, my experience showed me the mechanics of a small business and of business in general."

Which of the jobs you have held have you liked least?

It is likely that your work experience contained a certain amount of repetition and drudgery, as all early jobs in the business world do. So beware of saying that you hated a particular job "because it was boring." You'll also be knocked out of the running if your "least liked" matches up with the job's "most critical."

The job you liked least or what you liked least about a job, and how you express it, speaks of your willingness to take the ups and the downs that go with every job. Put your answer in the past; perhaps, "Burger King—hated smelling of French fries . . ." Then show that you learned, too. "When you get involved, there's always something to learn. I learned that . . ." End by moving the conversation forward, "Every job I've held has given me new insights into my profession. All my jobs had their good and bad points, but I've always found that if you want to learn, there's plenty to pick up every day. Each experience was valuable."

What are your future vocational plans?

This is a fancy way of asking, "Where do you want to be five years from now?" The mistake all entry-level professionals make is to say, "In management," because they think that shows drive and ambition. It has become such a trite answer, though, that it immediately generates a string of questions most recent graduates can't answer: What is a manager's job? What is a manager's prime responsibility? A manager in what area?

Your safest answer identifies you with the profession you are trying to break into and shows you have your feet on the ground: "I want to get ahead, and to do that I must be able to channel my energies and expertise into those areas that my industry and employer need. So in a couple of years I hope to have become a thorough professional with a clear understanding of the company, the industry, and where the biggest challenges and opportunities lie within my area of expertise. By that time, my goals for the future should be more sharply defined." An answer like that will set you far apart from your contemporaries.

What college did you attend, and why did you choose it?

The college you attended isn't as important as your reasons for choosing it—the question is trying to examine your reasoning processes. Emphasize that it was your choice, and that you didn't go there as a result of your parents' desires or because generations of your family have always attended the Acme School of Welding. Focus on the practical: "I went to Greenbriar State—it was a choice based on practicality. I wanted a school that would give me a good education and prepare me for the real world. State has a good record for turning out students fully prepared to take on responsibilities in the real world. It is [or isn't] a big school, and [or but] it has certainly taught me some big lessons about the value of [*transferable skills* and *professional values*] in the real world of business."

Are you looking for a permanent or temporary job?

This question is often asked of young candidates. The interviewer wants reassurance that you are genuinely interested in the position and won't disappear in a few months. Go beyond saying, "Permanent." Explain why you want the job: "Of course, I am looking for a permanent job. I intend to make my career in this field, and I want the opportunity to learn the business, face new challenges, and learn from experienced professionals like you." You will also want to qualify the question with one of your own: "Is this a permanent or a temporary position you are trying to fill?" Don't be scared to ask. The occasional unscrupulous employer will hire someone fresh out of school for a short period of time—say, for one particular project—then lay him off.

How did you pay for college?

Avoid saying, "Oh, Daddy handled all of that." Your parents may have helped you out, but if you can, emphasize that you worked part-time as much as you could. People who paid for their own education make big points with employers, because it shows *motivation*, and the experience always delivers a better grasp of the professional world. If this isn't you, find and listen to someone who can tell you what working in the professional world teaches you, and use the knowledge.

> *We have tried to hire people from your school/your major before, and they never seem to work out. What makes you different?*

This question examines your poise under pressure and *critical thinking skills*. It's often asked of candidates for sales jobs, where pressure situations have you thinking on your feet. However, you can't answer this question without more information. Respond this way: "First, may I ask you exactly what problems you've had with people from this school/background?" Once you know what the problem is (if one really exists at all—it may just be a curveball to test your poise), you can illustrate how you are different—but only then. Otherwise, you run the risk of your answer being interrupted with, "Well, that's what everyone else said before I hired them. You haven't shown me you are different."

> *I'd be interested to hear about some things you learned in school that could be used on the job.*

The interviewer wants to hear about "real-world" skills, so explain what the experience of college taught you about your profession and the professional world, rather than specific courses. You can use internships and any work experience to illustrate your points.

If you look back at college, you can find examples in every activity that gave you the opportunity to develop *transferable skills* and *professional values*. Your answer might say, in part, "Within academic and other on-campus activities, I always looked for the opportunity to apply and develop some of the practical skills demanded in the professional world, such as _____."

Do you like routine tasks/regular hours?

The interviewer knows from bitter experience that most recent graduates hate routine and are hopeless as employees until they come to an acceptance of such facts of life. Explain that, yes, you appreciate the need for routine, you expect a fair amount of routine assignments before you are entrusted with the more responsible ones, and that the routine and the repetitive always have a role in even the most creative of jobs. As far as regular hours go, you could say, "No, there's no problem there. A company expects to make a profit, so the doors have to be open for business on a regular basis."

What have you done that shows initiative and willingness to work?

You can tell a story about how you landed or created a job for yourself, or got involved in some volunteer work. Your answer should show that you both handled unexpected problems calmly and anticipated others. Your motivation is demonstrated by the ways you overcame obstacles. For example: "I worked for a summer in a small warehouse. I found out that a large shipment was due in a couple of weeks, and I knew that room had to be made. The inventory system was outdated, and the rear of the warehouse was disorganized, so I came in on a Saturday, figured out how much room I needed, cleaned up the mess in the rear, and cataloged it all on the new inventory forms. When the shipment arrived, the truck just backed in. There was even room to spare."

After your illustration, recap with something similar to, "I stick to my commitments. I am invested in doing good work and commit whatever time and effort is necessary to finish tasks properly, because I know other people's productivity depends on all aspects of my work being done properly."

Often, after an effort above and beyond the call of duty, a manager might congratulate you, and if it happened to you in this instance, you might conclude your answer with the verbal endorsement: "The divisional manager happened along just when I was finishing the job and said she wished she had more people who took such pride in their work."

Can you take instructions without feeling upset or hurt?

This is a manageability question. If you take offense easily or bristle when your mistakes are pointed out, you won't last long with any company. Competition is fierce at the entry level, so take this as another chance to set yourself apart: "Yes, I can take instruction—and more important, I can take constructive criticism without feeling hurt. Even with the best intent, I will still make mistakes, and at times someone will have to put me back on the right track. I know that if I'm ever to rise in the company, I must first prove myself to be manageable."

Have you ever had difficulties getting along with others?

This question examines your people skills and manageability. Are you a *team player*, or are you going to disrupt the department and make the manager's life miserable?

You can give a yes-or-no answer and shut up, but if you think through what you are going to say, your answer can also say something about your *professional values*. In this case, you say that there are two types in every department: the type who is engaged and committed to peak performance every day, and the type who does his job but without the same level of *commitment*. You can and do get on with everyone, but tend to bond more with the people who take a genuine *pride* in becoming their best.

What type of position are you interested in?

Another entry-level question that tempts you to mention management. Tell the interviewer you are interested in an entry-level job, which is what you will be offered anyway. "I am interested in an entry-level position that will enable me to learn this business from the ground up and will give me the opportunity to grow professionally once I prove myself."

What qualifications do you have that will make you successful in this field?

There is more to answering this question than reeling off your academic qualifications. In addition, you will want to stress relevant work experience and address the *transferable skills* and *professional values* you are developing as they relate to the target job. It's a wide-open question that says, "Hey, we're looking for an excuse to hire you. Give us some help."

Why do you think you would like this type of work?

This is a deceptive question because there is no pat answer. It is usually asked to see whether you really understand what the specific job entails on a day-to-day basis. Answering it requires careful research of the job, as suggested in the TJD discussion. It is also a good idea to network with people already in the profession engaged in exactly this target job. Ask what the job is like and what that person does day-to-day. How does the job fit into the department? What contribution does it make to the overall efforts of the company? Why does she like that type of work? Armed with this information, you will show that you understand what you are getting into; most recent graduates do not.

What's your idea of how this industry works?

The interviewer does not want a dissertation, just the reassurance that you don't think this company and the business world in general work along the same lines as a registered charity. Your understanding should be something like this: "The role of any company is to make as much money as possible, as quickly and efficiently as possible, and in a manner that will encourage repeat business from the existing client base and new business from word of mouth and reputation." Finish with the observation that it is every employee's role as a team member to help achieve those goals: "I am a small but important cog within this moneymaking machinery. I need to mesh well with the other cogs in my department so that we can collectively deliver on the department's responsibilities. On an individual basis, my job is to enhance productivity and profitability by the timely identification, anticipation, prevention, and solution of the problems that arise within my areas of professional expertise."

Why do you think this industry will sustain your interest over the long haul? Why do you think you will shine in this profession?

Your answer should speak to both your pragmatism and your motivation. "I am looking at the industry because I believe it offers stability and professional growth potential over the years [*explain why*]. Also, I'll be using skills [*itemize strong skill sets that are relevant to the job*] that are areas of strength, from which I derive great personal satisfaction."

What do you think determines progress in a good company?

Your answer will include a selection of *transferable skills* and *professional values* that are relevant to success in every company and profession. Begin with each of the *technical skills* you know are required to do the job, then follow with each of the other *transferable skills* that help you do the job well. Finish with reference to the *professional values* of integrity, commitment, a willingness to play by the rules, the ability to take the rough with the smooth, and the good fortune to have a manager who wants you to succeed.

Do you think grades should be considered by first employers?

If your grades were good, the answer is obviously "yes." If they weren't, your answer takes a little more thought: "Of course, an employer should take everything into consideration. Along with grades, there should be an evaluation of real *motivation* and manageability, an understanding of how business works, and actual work experience; plus, the best academics don't always make the most productive professionals. Einstein and Edison, two of the most intellectually and economically productive minds of modern times, had terrible academic records."

Many candidates are called for entry-level interviews, but only those who prepare themselves with an understanding of their target jobs will be chosen. Preparation takes time, so don't leave it until the last minute. You are taking a new product to market. Accordingly, you've got to analyze what it can do, who is likely to be interested, and how you are going to sell it to them. Start now and hone your skills to get a head start on your peers; you'll get more interviews, and the more you interview, the better you'll get.

CHAPTER 13

STRANGE VENUES FOR
JOB INTERVIEWS

WHY ARE SOME INTERVIEWS CONDUCTED IN STRANGE PLACES? Are meetings in noisy, distracting hotel lobbies designed as a form of torture? What are the real reasons that an interviewer invites you to eat at a fancy restaurant?

For the most part, these tough-on-the-nerves situations happen because the interviewer is a busy person, fitting you into a busy schedule. A woman I know had heard stories about tough interview situations but never expected to face one herself. It happened at a retail convention in Arizona, to which she had been asked for a final interview. The interview was conducted by the pool. The interviewer was there, taking a short break between meetings, in his bathing suit. The first thing the interviewer did was suggest that my friend slip into something comfortable.

That scenario may not lurk in your future, but the chances are you will face many tough interview situations in your career. They call for a clear head and a little gamesmanship if you want to stay ahead of the competition. The interviewee at the pool used both. She removed her jacket, folded it over the arm of the chair, and seated herself, saying pleasantly, "That's much better. Where shall we begin?"

It isn't easy to remain calm at such times. On top of interview nerves, you're worried about being overheard in a public place, or (worse) surprised by the appearance of your current boss. That last item isn't too far-fetched. It actually happened to a reader from San Francisco. He was being interviewed in the departure lounge at the airport when his boss walked through the arrivals door. Oops—he had asked for the day off "to go to the doctor."

Could he have avoided the situation? Certainly, if he had asked about privacy when the meeting was arranged. That would have reminded the interviewer of the need for discretion. The point is to do all you can in advance to make such a meeting as private as possible. Once that's done, you can ignore the rest of the world and concentrate on the interviewer's questions.

Hotel Lobbies and Other Strange Places

Strange interview situations provide other wonderful opportunities to embarrass yourself. You come to a hotel lobby in full corporate battle dress and you sit down to wait for the interviewer. "Aha," you think to yourself, opening your briefcase, "I'll show him my excellent work habits by noodling around on my laptop."

That's not such a great idea. Have you ever tried rising with your lap covered with a laptop or business papers, then juggling the briefcase from right hand to left to accommodate the ritual handshake? It's quite difficult. If you have to read something, make it your resume or the list of questions you developed; both activities will help immerse yourself in the professional you.

Besides, while you are sitting in nervous anticipation, pre-interview tension has no way of dissipating. Your mouth will become dry, and your "Good morning, I'm pleased to meet you" will come out sounding like a cat being strangled.

To avoid such catastrophes in places like hotel lobbies, instead of sitting, walk around a little while you wait. Even in a small lobby, a few steps back and forth will help you reduce tension to a manageable level. If you carry a briefcase, keep it with you at all times: It makes you look purposeful, and you won't trip over it when you meet the interviewer.

If for any reason you must sit, breathe deeply and slowly. This will help control the adrenaline that makes you feel jumpy.

A strange setting can actually put you on equal footing with the interviewer. Neither of you is on home turf, so in many cases the interviewer will feel just as awkward as you do. A little gamesmanship can turn the occasion to your advantage.

To gain the upper hand, get to the meeting site early to scout the territory. By knowing your surroundings, you will feel more relaxed. Early arrival also allows you to control the outcome of the meeting in other subtle ways. You will have time to stake out the most private spot in an otherwise public place. Corners are best. They tend to be quieter, and you can choose the seat that puts your back to the wall (in a physical sense, that is). In this position, you have a clear view of your surroundings and will feel more secure. The fear of being overheard will evaporate.

The situation is now somewhat favorable. You know the locale, and the meeting place is as much yours as the interviewer's. You will have a clear view of your surroundings, and odds are that you will be more relaxed than the interviewer. When she arrives, say, "I arrived a little early to make sure we had some privacy. I think over here is the best spot." With that positive demonstration of your organizational abilities, you give yourself a head start over the competition.

The Meal Meeting

Breakfast, lunch, and dinner are the prime choices for interviewers who want to catch the seasoned professional off guard. In fact, the meal is arguably the toughest of all tough interview situations. The setting offers the interviewer the chance to see you in a nonoffice (and therefore more natural) setting, to observe your social graces, and to consider you as a whole person. Here, topics that would be impossible to address in the traditional office setting will surface, often with virtually no effort on the part of the interviewer. The slightest slip in front of that wily old pirate (thinly disguised in a Brooks Brothers suit) could get your candidacy deep-sixed in a hurry.

Usually you will not be invited to a "meal meeting" until you have already demonstrated that you are capable of doing the job. An invitation to a meal means that you are under strong consideration, and therefore intense scrutiny.

This meeting is often the final hurdle and could lead directly to the job offer—assuming that you properly handle the occasional surprises that arise. The interviewer's concern is not whether you can do the job, but whether you have the growth potential that will allow you to fill more senior slots as they become available.

But be careful. Many have fallen at the final hurdle in a close-run race. Being interviewed in front of others is bad enough; eating and drinking in front of them at the same time only makes it worse. If you knock over a glass or dribble spaghetti sauce down your chin, the interviewer will be so busy smirking that he won't hear what you have to say.

To be sure that he remains as attentive to the positive points of your candidacy as possible, let's discuss table manners.

Your social graces and general demeanor at the table can reveal as much about you as your answer to a question. For instance, over-ordering food or drink can signal poor self-discipline. At the very least, it will call into question your judgment and maturity. High-handed behavior toward waiters and busboys could reflect negatively on your ability to get along with subordinates and on your *leadership skills*. Those concerns are amplified when you return food or complain about the service, actions which, at the very least, find fault with the interviewer's choice of restaurant.

By the same token, you will want to observe how your potential employer behaves. After all, you are likely to become an employee, and the interviewer's behavior to servers in a restaurant can tell you a lot about what it will be like on the job.

Here are some specific tips:

- **Alcohol:** Soon after being seated, you will be offered a drink—if not by your host, then by the waiter. There are many reasons to avoid alcohol at interview meals. The most important reason is that alcohol fuzzes your mind, and research proves that stress increases the intoxicating effect of alcohol. So, if you order something to drink, stick with something nonalcoholic, such as a club soda, Coke or Pepsi, or simply a glass of water.

   If you do have a drink, never have more than one. If there is a bottle of wine on the table, and the waiter offers you another glass, place your hand over the top of your glass. It is a polite way of signifying no.

   You may be offered alcohol at the end of the meal. The rule still holds true—turn it down. You need your wits about you, even if the interview seems to be drawing to a close. Some interviewers will try to use those moments, when your defenses are at their lowest, to throw in a couple of zingers.
- **Smoking:** Don't smoke under any circumstances.
- **Utensils:** Keep all your cups and glasses at the top of your place setting and well away from you. Glasses are knocked over at a cluttered table most often when one stretches for the condiments or gesticulates to make a point.

Here are some other helpful hints:

- Never speak with your mouth full.
- Order something that is easy to eat, as you are there for talking, not eating.
- Do not change your order once it is made, and never send the food back.
- Be polite to your waiters, even when they spill soup in your lap.
- Don't order expensive food. Naturally, in our heart of hearts, we all like to eat well, especially on someone else's tab. But don't be tempted. When you come right down to it, you are there to talk and be seen at your best, not to eat.

- Eat what you know. Stay away from awkward, messy, or exotic foods (e.g., artichokes, long pasta, and escargot, respectively). Ignore finger foods, such as lobster or spare ribs. In fact, you should avoid eating with your fingers altogether, unless you are in a sandwich joint, in which case you should make a point of avoiding the leaky, overstuffed menu items.
- Don't order salad. The dressing can often get messy. If a salad comes with the meal, request that the dressing be on the side. Then, before pouring it on, cut up the lettuce.
- Don't order anything with bones. Stick with fillets; there are few simple, gracious ways to deal with any type of bone.
- Checks and Goodbyes: I know an interviewer whose favorite test of composure is to have the waiter, by arrangement, put the bill on the interviewee's side of the table. She then chats on, waiting for something interesting to happen. If you ever find yourself in a similar situation, never pick up the check, however long it is left by your plate. When ready, your host will pick it up, because that's the protocol of the occasion. By the same token, you should never offer to share payment.

When parting company, always thank the host for her hospitality and the wonderful meal. Of course, you should be sure to leave on a positive note by asking good-naturedly what you have to do to get the job.

Strange interview situations can arise at any time during the interview cycle, and in any public place. Wherever you are asked to go, keep your guard up. Your table manners, listening skills, and overall social graces are being judged. The question on the interviewer's mind is: Can you be trusted to represent the company gracefully and with a professional demeanor?

Wherever the interview occurs, it will come to an end, and you need to end on a high note that leads to the next interview and the job offer . . .

CHAPTER 14

THE GRACEFUL EXIT

To paraphrase Shakespeare, all the working world's a stage. Curtains rise and fall, and your powerful interview performance must be capped with a professional and memorable exit. To ensure that you leave the right impression, this chapter reviews the dos and don'ts of leaving an interview.

A signal that the interview is drawing to a close comes when you are asked if you have any questions. Ask questions, and by doing so, highlight your strengths and show your enthusiasm. Remember, your goal at the interview is to generate a job offer. Make sure your exit is as graceful as your entrance.

Dos:

1. *When more than one person interviews you, be sure you have the correct spellings of their names.* "I enjoyed meeting your colleagues, Ms. Smith. Could you give me the correct spellings of their names, please?" This question will give you the names if you forget them in the heat of battle, and it will demonstrate your consideration.

2. *Ask appropriate job-related questions.* When the opportunity comes to ask any final questions, remember that your candidacy is evaluated partly by the statements you make but also partly by the questions you ask, because those questions can demonstrate the depth of your understanding of the job. If you haven't asked before:

- "Who succeeds in this job and why?"
- "Who fails in this job and why?"
- "What do you consider the most important day-to-day responsibilities of this job?" "What are the most common day-to-day problems of the job, and how do your best people execute their work to prevent these problems from arising?"
- "What is the hardest part of the job?"
- "Which projects will I be most involved with during the first six months?"
- "What will you want me to have achieved after ninety days?"
- "What will you want me to have achieved after six months?"
- "What are the biggest challenges the department faces this year and what will be my role as a team member in tackling them?"
- "What skills and values do you consider critical to success in this job?"

    The information gathered from questions like these will help you make a strong closing argument for your candidacy.

3. *Review the job's requirements with the interviewer.* Match them point-by-point with your skills and attributes.

4. *Determine next steps.* If there are more interviews in the selection cycle, express your interest, recap why you feel qualified for the job, and *ask* for that next interview, "Is now a good time to schedule our next meeting?"

    If there are no more interviews, find out the time frame for a decision and *ask for the job* in a positive and enthusiastic manner. Recap for the interviewer why you are qualified for the job, what kind of contributions you can make, why you would like to join the company and the team, and finish by saying, "I am excited by this job and the prospect of becoming part of your team. I guess the only question I have now is, what do I have to do to get a job offer?" or, "I am very enthusiastic about the job and the contributions I can make. If your decision will be made by the fifteenth, what must I do in the meantime to ensure I get the job?" And then you smile.

Hiring managers want to hire someone who is *intelligently enthusiastic* about the job and about joining the team. Any head-hunter will tell you—and they sit in the middle of hundreds of negotiations every year—that when there is nothing to choose between two candidates, the offer always goes to the one who is most *intelligently enthusiastic*.

5. *Show decisiveness.* If you are offered the job, react with enthusiasm, but before making any commitment, read the next chapter.

Don'ts:

1. *Don't discuss salary, vacation, or benefits.* It is not that the questions are invalid, just that the timing is wrong. Bringing up such topics before you have an offer is asking what the company can do for you—instead, you should be saying what you can do for the company. Negotiations follow the job offer; they don't precede it.

2. *Don't press for an early decision.* Of course, you should ask, "When will I know your decision?" But don't try to use the "other opportunities I have to consider" gambit as leverage when no such offers exist—that annoys the interviewer, makes you look foolish, and may even force you to negotiate from a position of weakness.

3. *Don't show discouragement.* Sometimes a job offer can occur on the spot. Usually it does not. So don't show discouragement if you are not offered the job at the interview, because discouragement shows

a lack of self-esteem and determination. Avoiding a bad impression is the foundation of leaving a good one, and the right image to leave is one of enthusiasm, guts, and openness—just the professional behaviors you have been projecting throughout the interview.

4. *Don't ask for an evaluation of your interview performance.* That forces the issue and puts the interviewer in an awkward position.

As You Are Leaving

Always depart in the same polite and assured manner with which you entered. Look the interviewer in the eye, smile, give a firm handshake, and say, "This has been an exciting meeting for me. This is a job I can do, and I feel I can contribute to your goals, because the atmosphere here seems conducive to doing my very best work. When will we speak again?" Another good parting question to ask is, "Until I hear from you again, what particular aspects of the job and this interview should I be considering?"

CHAPTER 15

How to Ace the Psychological Tests

Employers increasingly use psychological tests as part of the selection process. These tests may be known as aptitude tests; personality profiles; personnel selection tests; or skills, aptitude, and integrity tests, but in the end they are all the same thing: an attempt to find out if you show signs of being a "risky" hire.

It isn't surprising that many of the companies using the tests are concerned about the honesty of prospective employees. Each year, American business loses an estimated $40 billion to employee theft. While honesty is often one of the behavioral profiles examined, the tests can also examine aptitude and suitability for a position. These tests can evaluate the amount of energy a person might bring to the job, how she would handle stress, and what her attitudes toward job, peers, and management would be. Psychological tests are usually encountered as multiple-choice written tests.

We Are All Professional Schizophrenics

I once did an in-house employee selection and motivation seminar for a large corporation in Australia. They had a test that was "virtually infallible" in helping to identify strong hires, and asked if I would be prepared to take it. "Let me take the test twice," I said. "The first profile you get will tell you to hire me; the second will say I'm a bad risk."

I took the test twice that day. "Applicant #1" came back with a strong recommendation for hire. "Applicant #2" came back with a warning to exercise caution.

How was this possible? Well, none of us is the same person in the workplace as in our personal life. Over a period of time at work, we come to understand the need for different behavioral patterns and different ways of interacting with people. As professionals, we are inculcated with a set of behavioral patterns that make us successful and productive for our employers. In the world of work, we are not expected to override the "professional way" of doing things according to our personal preferences. When personal preferences take precedence over professional standards of behavior, we get warnings and terminations.

Did I really "fool" the test? No. I was completely honest both times. The "winning" test was the one in which I viewed myself—and, thus, described myself—as a thoroughly professional white-collar worker in the job for which I was applying. The "losing" test was the one I used to describe myself as the kind of person I see myself as in my personal life.

I am that person they would have hired, and I did possess a strong track record to back up the test results. I have learned the behaviors necessary to succeed in the professional world and made them my own—just as you have undoubtedly done, or are in the process of doing.

Many of the tests lack an awareness of the complexity of the human mind. They seem to miss the point when they ask us to speak honestly about our feelings and beliefs. They do not take into account that our learned behaviors in our professional lives are, invariably, distinct from the behaviors we display in our personal lives.

If you understand what you are likely to face, you can prepare and present yourself in the most effective way, and you can do it without compromising your integrity.

How to Prepare for, Read, and Answer the Tests

There are five different types of tests, designed to plumb different aspects of your doubtless troubled psyche:

- Personality
- Personnel selection
- Aptitude
- Skills
- Integrity

Let's take a look at each of these.

Personality Tests

Are you a people person? Do you get upset easily? Are you quick to anger? Employers are using tests of general personality more frequently these days to screen job candidates. They use these tests because they believe that certain personality traits are required for success in a particular position.

There are two basic kinds of personality tests: projective and objective.

Projective Personality Tests. The projective tests ask you to tell a story, finish a sentence, or describe what you see in a blob of ink. These tests, in some form or other, have been around for decades, and psychologists use them a great deal to help understand how we deal with tough issues.

One popular test shows you pictures of a scene and asks you to describe what's going on. The psychologist may ask you to "tell me more about it." These areas of your mind are also accessed through the use of incomplete sentences, where you are given the beginning of a sentence and have to fill in the rest of it on your own. So, for instance, you may be asked to complete a sentence such as "When I am at work, I . . ."

In an employment-selection context, these tests are generally looking for leaders, achievers, and winners. They search for analytical and system-thinking skills, and look at decision-making and consensus-building styles.

Objective Personality Tests. Objective personality tests ask dozens, sometimes hundreds, of questions using some sort of rating scale, like strongly agree to strongly disagree, true-or-false, or yes-or-no. These tests usually have good reliability and validity. They were not designed to be used for employee screening, although they often are.

Knowing the names of the most common tests can tip you off to the type of screening being done, and often an Internet search can lead you to practice sites. Tests you might run into that screen personality include:

- *NEO Personality Inventory*: measures adjustment, extroversion, openness, agreeability, and conscientiousness.
- *16 PF*: measures sixteen personality factors, including a lie scale.
- *California Psychological Inventory*: measures twenty personality scales such as empathy, tolerance, responsibility, and dominance. (This is a good personality test, but it can be expensive for an employer, so it isn't used as often as some others.)
- *Minnesota Multiphasic Personality Inventory*: a very long, heavy-duty test of major psychological problems, often (wrongly) used in employee selection.

Personnel Selection Tests

Personnel selection tests are personality tests designed specifically to screen job candidates. These tests measure psychological behaviors such as trustworthiness, reliability, and conscientiousness. Some of them also psychologically screen you for potential alcohol or substance abuse. Tests you might run into that examine these areas include:

- Hogan Personality Inventory
- Employee Reliability Inventory
- PDI Employment Inventory

Aptitude

If you don't have the skills it takes to do the job, do you have the aptitude to learn? In a work world where the learning curve for new skill development becomes increasingly interesting to potential employers, we can expect to see the use of aptitude tests on the upswing. Judging your ability to develop skills in general or skills in a particular area is the premise behind these aptitude tests.

Some of the aptitude tests you might run into that examine these areas include:

- Wechsler Adult Intelligence Scale—Revised
- Raven's Progressive Matrices
- Comprehensive Ability Battery
- Differential Aptitude Tests

Skills

If the job calls for typing seventy five words per minute, you may be given a typing test. If you are a programmer, you may be asked to take an objective test of programming skills or debug a program. There are tests to measure every possible skill: filing, bookkeeping, mechanical comprehension, specific computer programs, math, credit rating, and so on. Some of them are typical paper-and-pencil written tests. Newer tests present the information using a software program.

It's hard to argue against some of these tests. After all, if the job calls for you to type letters and reports all day, the employer wants to hire the best typist. If you're supposed to use Microsoft Word on a PC all day, the employer will look for the person with the best knowledge of that program. As long as the employer is measuring an important skill, testing skills makes sense.

Integrity Tests

Integrity tests are increasingly popular. Some companies are leery of personality tests, so they turn to integrity tests to screen out liars, cheats, and thieves. Some tests measure honesty, or integrity, whereas others measure other psychological traits.

The problem with these integrity tests is that they don't work. A psychologist wrote that in one case using an integrity test would eliminate 2,721 honest applicants so that 101 potentially dishonest applicants would be denied employment. The integrity test itself actually is okay; it's just that so few people actually steal that the use of the test eliminates a heck of a lot of good applicants. Another major study found that 95.6 percent of people who take these tests and get a failing score are actually incorrectly classified!

Here are a couple of integrity tests in consistent use today:

- Personnel Selection Inventory
- Personnel Reaction Bank

Listen carefully and apply what you learn in this chapter so that you don't become an incorrectly classified statistic.

Getting to Know Yourself and Acing the Mind Readers

If we were all independently wealthy, very few of us would be doing the jobs we do. But we are doing them, and we have learned certain sets of skills and behavioral traits that are critical to our ability to survive and succeed professionally. The first thing you must do, then, is identify and separate the professional you from the personal you.

1. **Step One:** Never answer a test question from the viewpoint of your innermost beliefs. Instead, use your learned and developed professional behavior traits and *modus operandi*. Ask yourself, "How has my experience as a professional taught me to think and respond to this?" To do this effectively (and to understand ourselves a little better in the process), we need some further insights into the critical skill sets that every professional relies on to succeed:

- *Professional/technical skills* (whether you're a secretary or a senior vice president). These include the *technical skills* of the job, and the *transferable skills* that give you the ability to do your work well.
- *Industry skills* (such as—if you happen to be in banking—your overall knowledge of the world of banking: how things work, how things get done, what is accepted within the industry, and so on).

2. **Step Two:** Look at yourself from the employer's point of view. Review Chapter 1 and Chapter 8 for some helpful ideas. Evaluate the traits that enable you to discharge your duties effectively. Examine the typical crises/emergencies likely to arise: What supportive behavioral traits are necessary to overcome them? As you do this, you will almost certainly relive some episodes that seemed to put you at a disadvantage for a time. When it was tough to do things the right way, you had to buckle down and see the problem through, even though doing so did not necessarily "come naturally." The fact is, though, you overcame the obstacle. Remember how you did so, and keep that in mind as you answer the questions.

    Conversely, you will want to look at those instances where a crisis had a less-than-successful outcome. What traits did you swear you would develop and use for next time?

    Highlighting such traits constitutes your acknowledgment of the supremacy of learned behavior in the workplace. It does *not* constitute lying. Why do you think so many professionals strive to keep their business lives separate from their personal lives? What is the point of such a separation if the two lives are identical?

3. **Step Three:** Think of people you've known who have failed on the job. Why did they fail? What have you learned from their mistakes and made a part of the "professional you"?

4. **Step Four:** Think of people you've known who have succeeded on the job. Why did they succeed? What have you learned from their success and made a part of the "professional you"?

Once you have completed this exercise in detail, you will have determined how a professional would react in a wide range of circumstances, and identified the ways in which you have, over time, developed a "professional self" to match that profile.

Getting Ready for the Test

Any test can be nerve-wracking, but when it comes to these tests your livelihood is in the balance, so tip the odds in your favor with these tried and proven techniques:

- The tests instruct you to answer quickly, offering the first response that comes to mind. Don't. Following this path may cost you a job. Instead, look at the test in terms of the exercises outlined above; provide reasoned responses from the viewpoint of the "professional you."
- Time limits are usually not imposed. On the contrary, those administering the test will often begin the proceedings with a soothing "take your time, there's no pressure." (Except, of course, the minor pressure of knowing a job offer is on the line!)
- If there is a time limit, find out how much time you have. Figure out about how much time per question or section you have. Pacing yourself helps, because then you won't panic when you realize you've only got five minutes to complete the second half of a fifteen-minute test. Of course, you'll bring your watch.
- Answer the questions you can, but don't dwell on the ones you can't. Mark the ones you can't and come back to them later.
- When in doubt, guess. Some of the really sophisticated tests you may have taken to get into college nailed you if you guessed wrong, but skill tests usually work differently. They add up all your right answers to get your test score. So, when in doubt, eliminate any of the obviously wrong answers, and take your best shot.

- With skill tests, ask for a warmup or practice section. One computer-typing test has an optional practice session. Ask about it. If the test is on a computer, adjust your chair, keyboard, and monitor before the timer starts.
- For paper and pencil tests, make sure you have enough desk space and sharp pencils.
- If the test is going to be done with other applicants in a group situation, stay focused on what you are doing. If you have to sit in the front of the room so no one else distracts you, do it. If the test will be long and there's no break, make sure you won't get hungry (take a PowerBar) or have to use the bathroom.
- No matter what, use all your allotted time! Check your answers; make sure that they are written in the right places and that the right boxes are checked. Depending on your remaining time, review every other, or every fourth, question. Of course, if you can recall at the end which questions you were unsure about, review those first.
- You may not even realize you're taking an integrity test until the direction of the questions gives it away: "Have you ever stolen anything?" "Have you ever felt guilty?" "Have you ever told a lie?" Avoid the temptation to respond impulsively with something like "Lies? No, I prefer to chop down the damned cherry tree." The truth is, we have all done these things in our lives. When you are asked, for instance, whether there is anything you would ever change about yourself, or whether you think everyone is dishonest to some degree, the overwhelming likelihood is that your own honesty is being tested: The best answer is probably "yes."

In fact, if you never admit to these behaviors, you could be pegged as a faker. While fakers may be kept in the running, they've earned a question mark. Fakers are sometimes viewed as being eager to please or simply a bit out of touch with their true feelings.

Many of the better tests in use today also use lie scales that can detect when someone is faking. How do they do this? One way is to include questions like, "I always tell the truth" or "I never have a negative thought about a coworker." When the test is developed, hundreds or thousands of people take it, and the researchers figure out what the typical response is to these questions. Anyone who deviates from the average response on enough of these faking questions is also flagged as a faker.

If you must answer questions about ethics in a face-to-face encounter, explain your answer, placing it far in the past when appropriate, and explain what you have learned from any negative experience. If such questions must be answered on paper, the best approach is to follow the dictates of your own conscience and try to bring up the issue after the test. You might say something like this:

"Gee, that question about lying was a tough one. I guess everyone has told a lie at some time in the past, and I wanted to be truthful, so I said 'yes.' But I'd be lying if I didn't tell you it made me nervous. You know, I saw a show on television recently about these tests. It told the story of someone who lost a job because of answering a question just like that; the profile came back with an untrustworthy rating."

This may reduce the odds of your being denied the job in the same way. If the test does come back with a question about your honesty, you will at least have sown seeds of doubt about the validity of such a rating in the interviewer's mind. That doubt, and your disarming honesty, might just turn the tables in your favor.

Be careful, and take a balanced approach as you answer integrity test questions. Honesty is the best policy:

- The test may contain "double blinds," where you are asked a question on page one, and then asked a virtually identical one thirty or forty questions later. The technique is based on the belief that most of us can tell a lie, but few of us can remember that lie under stress, and are therefore likely to answer differently later. Thus, the duplicate questions aim to show the potential for untruthfulness. The problem isn't that one answer is likely to deny you employment; the questions are asked in patterns to evaluate your behavior and attitudes on different topics.
- Read the test through before you start answering questions! (There's "plenty of time" and "no pressure," remember?) Review the mate-

rial at least three times, mentally flagging the questions that seem similar. This way you will be able to answer consistently.

- Resist any temptation to project an image of yourself as an interesting person. These tests are not designed to reward eccentricity: Think sliced white bread. You are happy at work and home. You enjoy being around people. You don't spend all your evenings watching movies. You don't spend your weekends with a computer or pursuing other solitary pastimes (unless you are a programmer or an aspiring Trappist monk). You have beliefs, but not too strong. You respect the beliefs of all others, regardless of their age, sex, race, or religion.

- Relax. One part of the Wechsler test (a developmental aptitude test) asks you to repeat back a string of numbers to the psychologist. If you're too hyped up, you'll get flustered and blow it. These tests measure intelligence plus your test-taking behavior. And you can certainly improve your test-taking behavior!

- If tests make you nervous, it is a good idea to take advantage of the many test-practice resources available on the Internet; try keyword searches like, "Test-taking practice" or "Test-taking resources."

- Learn to visualize success in advance. Picture yourself at the test. Go through each step: You hear the instructions; the examiner says, "Begin." You read the test questions and realize you will do well. You get to a really tough part of the test. Visualize your success, and visualize your setbacks. Realize that you can and you will pull through okay because you have a clear vision of the professional you. When you finish the test, read through your answers a few times. If you don't like any answers, change them.

- Remember to use your professional, working mindset when you take these tests. Answer as you would if you were on the job and your boss were asking the questions.

It is important to separate the *professional you* from the personal you in everything you do in your work, but nowhere is it more important than in taking these tests. When you have learned to behave in ways that help you prosper in your profession, it is your right to provide an honest profile of your professional self.

PART FOUR

SEALING THE DEAL

CHAPTER 16

OUT OF SIGHT CAN MEAN OUT OF MIND

FOLLOW-UP AFTER AN INTERVIEW IS A CRITICAL STEP in winning any job offer, but the longer the decision-making period, the less distinct candidates become from each other in the hiring manager's memory. You leave your interviewers with a strong, positive image, and you don't want that memory to slip with the passage of time and a busy schedule.

We've noted that in tightly run job races, the offer invariably goes to the candidate who is most *intelligently enthusiastic*; following up on your interviews demonstrates this *intelligent enthusiasm* and is noted both in the breach and the observance. If you develop a consistent strategy to keep your name and skills constantly in the forefront of every interviewer's mind, it can make the difference between receiving an offer and not.

As soon as you can after the interview, make notes on what happened. Make notes on these categories:

- Who did you meet? What were their titles and e-mail addresses?
- What did you find out about the job?
- What are its first projects/challenges?
- Why can you do it? What are the problems?
- What went right and why?

- What went less well?
- What did the interviewer say on any topic related to the job, company, competition, industry, or profession that might give you a unique follow-up, were you to Google something interesting?
- What was a royal screwup and why?
- What did the interviewer say was the next step?
- Are there other candidates in contention?
- When will a decision be made?
- What did the interviewer say in concluding the interview?

Reviewing all your follow-up notes after two or three interviews may alert you to a weakness you hadn't noticed. Self-awareness, that rare ability to look at oneself objectively, is always the first step in fixing interview performance problems that come between you and job offers.

Using the information gathered from this exercise, you can begin a follow-up campaign.

Follow-Up Steps and Pacing

Knowing where you are in the selection cycle will help you execute a well-paced follow-up campaign.

If this is the final interview and the decision is imminent, you should follow up within twenty-four hours, or sooner, as the timeframe demands.

When the decision isn't going to be made in the next seventy-two hours—and most of the time it won't be, because there can be one, two, three, or more interviews to go through—a differently paced schedule is called for. In these instances, you start with an informal follow-up within twenty-four hours, followed by a well-considered e-mail or letter arriving two or three days later. This will re-energize your candidacy just when it was beginning to slip from memory.

We'll start with follow-up after the first interview in a series of interviews, and work chronologically toward follow-up as offer time becomes imminent.

After the First Interview in a Cycle
INFORMAL FIRST FOLLOW-UP WITHIN TWENTY-FOUR HOURS

If you can find something interesting related to the job, company, competition, industry, or profession, your first follow-up will be professional-casual, reinforcing the tone of an ongoing conversation between two professionals with a common interest. You'll send an e-mail that opens with a salutation: "Hi John/Jane," if you are close enough in years and experience to use first names. If you are younger and have been encouraged to use first names, it's okay too, but reverting to the formalities of Mr./Ms. in written communication (until after the second meeting), will usually be received as respectful and flattering. If use of first names hasn't been encouraged, don't presume: It won't win you points, while showing professional courtesies always does.

When time allows, follow-up e-mails and letters are especially powerful, because they can be referred back to, and are often stored with other documents relevant to your candidacy. Plus, the written word stays in the memory longer and with greater clarity than conversations.

This tactic first requires that you have a stack of profession/industry/job-related articles of weight. Note the short, punchy, casual yet professional tone of this follow-up e-mail·

"It was great to meet you this afternoon. I really enjoyed talking about the _____ position. Our conversation on _____ has been buzzing in the back of my mind all day. I just ran across this article (see attachment) and knew you'd enjoy it. On a deadline, so I'll follow up properly as soon as my schedule permits.

Best,

Martin Yate"

Send the first follow-up e-mail between 7:00 P.M. and 10:00 P.M. that evening or early the next morning when you first get up. You want the employer to see you enthusiastic and thinking about the job outside of normal business hours. Do not send an e-mail during business hours, for obvious reasons.

Assuming you are professionally competent to begin with, and have bought into the *Knock 'em Dead* philosophy and applied it to your job interviews, your first meeting will have tagged you as someone different. This initial follow-up aims to continue the differentiation. The tone is respectful, and shows a committed professional working late (you can't write fully because you are working on a deadline) who is *intelligently enthusiastic* (you are actively engaged in thinking about this job and your profession outside of business hours).

FORMAL FIRST FOLLOW-UP

Your formal first follow-up should arrive two to three days after the first interview, or after your first *informal* follow-up; adjusting your timing to the needs of the selection cycle for that particular job. This formal follow-up letter should make the following points:

- The date and time you met with the interviewer and the title of the target job
- You paid attention to what was said in the interview
- Why you can do the job
- You are excited about the job and want it
- You have the experience to contribute to those first major projects as discussed in the interview

ADDING NEW INFORMATION

Your follow-up note is also a good opportunity to add new information that you realize would be relevant, to answer any questions you didn't adequately address, or to introduce any aspects of your experience that you forgot in the heat of the moment. You can say something along the lines of, "On reflection, I . . . " or "Having thought about our meeting, I thought I'd mention . . . " or "I should have mentioned that . . . "

Keep the note short (less than one page) and address it to the hiring manager or main interviewer if you haven't met your new boss yet. If you interviewed with other people and the meeting was more than cursory you can send separate e-mails to each.

Additional Interviews

Sometimes, of course, the hiring cycle has to work its way through three or more interviews for a handful of candidates, and this can take a while. This can be exacerbated during recessions or recovering economic downturns: Managers are short-handed and overworked, budgets are tight, and there is more hesitancy before the company makes its final hiring decision.

If the selection cycle is normal, three typical interviews can take about three weeks, so with the second and subsequent interviews (excepting the final interview), your follow-up pattern should replicate the follow-up pattern from the initial interview.

If the process stretches out into a month or months, make contact every couple of weeks, but keep it very low-volume. You don't want to seem overly anxious, just interested.

1. Make an informal follow-up within twenty-four hours, even shorter and simply saying in your own words:

    "Good to see you again, Jack. Thanks for your time. Preparing for a client meeting; I'll get back to you properly in the next couple of days."

    You might replace this with an equally brief phone call and, if the manager doesn't pick up, leave a complete message.

2. Make a formal follow-up, following the same principles and timing as before, except that you need not mention the date/time and the job you are interviewing for. As the interview cycle progresses, you want to maintain awareness of your candidacy,

but you don't want to be seen as doing anything by rote. You might consider sending profession-relevant information:

"Harry, being so busy, you may not have seen the article I've attached. It's about new legislation that's bound to affect us.
Regards,
Martin
P.S. I'm still determined to be your next _____."

3. Extended Interview Cycles: You don't want to make a pest of yourself by calling or e-mailing every day, but neither do you want to drop out of sight. If the process stretches out into a month or months, make contact every couple of weeks, but, again, keep it very low-volume. You don't want to seem overly anxious, just interested.

As you did once before, you might send timely and profession-relevant information:

"Harry, here's a link to a blog about legislation that could affect our profession.
Regards,
Martin
P.S. I'm still determined to be your next _____."

You can do this in an e-mail and/or by traditional mail. Getting a funny e-mail always brightens the day, and giving the interviewer a smile is a great way to be remembered, but this requires judgment. You cannot send anything of a sexual, political, or religious nature, as it constitutes a breach of *professional values*.

Sending a cartoon via traditional mail works because it's a different delivery medium and the cartoon causes a smile; plus, if you're lucky, the cartoon gets stuck on the wall or passed on.

Reposted Jobs

Sometimes jobs remain open for a long time, or they may be frozen because of budgetary constraints and reposted under a different job title. In these instances, go through an attenuated TJD exercise with the new job title to make sure the job hasn't changed in any meaningful ways, and that you still have all the relevant keywords. If you're still in touch with the hiring manager or recruiter, send them the customized and updated version of your resume, noting the changes in their needs, then make a follow-up call.

Keep in mind a sad fact of life: The longer the hiring process drags on, the less likely it is that you will get the offer. It can happen, but the odds get longer as time goes by. Don't let your job search stand still while you're waiting for a response from one company. Remember: *You don't have the job until you have a written offer in hand.*

When the Hiring Decision Is Imminent

If you know in advance that a decision is coming, say Friday of the following week, you can aim to get an e-mail on the hiring manager's desk this Friday/Monday; a slight variation of that message might arrive via traditional mail on the same day or Tuesday; and you can make a telephone call no later than Wednesday morning. This leaves seventy-two hours before decision time; based on my experience over the years, a decision next Friday means that an offer will be extended on that date, while the actual decision is often made *at least* seventy-two hours to five days prior, allowing HR the time to shepherd the decision through the authorization process. This is usually the case when your last interview is a week or more in advance of the announced decision date. Of course, if you are interviewing for a job today and they tell you the decision will be made at the end of the week, it *isn't* the case, and as always you adapt follow-up strategy to reflect the demands of the hiring cycle.

Final Written Communications

The content of these communications should cover:

- "We last met on _____ and have been talking about _____ job."
- "I can do the job and this is why: [talk about the *technical skills* you bring]."
- "I am excited about the job and this is why: [talk about how you can contribute to first projects and your desire to join a great group of people]."
- "I will make a good hire and this is why: [talk about the *transferable skills* and *professional values* you bring to the job]."
- "I want the job. What do I have to do to get it?"

Making That Final Call

If a hiring decision is imminent, succinctly following up on your e-mails and letters within seventy-two hours of decision time might help seal the deal. Work out what you want to say, write it down in bullet points, and make practice calls to friends, keeping it brief and to the point. Then, when you are ready make the call, you have nothing to lose and a job offer to gain.

CHAPTER 17

NEGOTIATING THE JOB OFFER

A JOB OFFER WILL EVENTUALLY BE PUT ON THE TABLE, often after one or two approach questions about money.

Here are some end-of-the-line questions you might be asked.

Why should I hire you?

Keep your answer short and to the point. Demonstrate your grasp of the job's responsibilities, the problems typically occurring in each area, the *transferable skills* that allow you to consistently deliver on them, and then a brief review of what you are like as a professional colleague, personalizing the behavioral profile for success you identified in your *TJD*.

You might finish with a comment that says, in effect, "I have the qualifications you need [*itemize them*], I'm a team player, I take direction well, and I am committed to success."

What are you earning currently?/What were you making on your last job?

Ideally, the offer you negotiate should be based on salary norms (do your research) and on the value you bring to the job. However, all too often an employer will want to base any forthcoming offer on your current salary.

If you are currently well remunerated and just want a nice bump with your job change, this isn't a problem, but if you are underpaid it's a different situation. You might consider saying, "I am earning _____, but I want you to know that a major reason for making a job change right now is to significantly increase my salary. I am currently underpaid for my skills, experience, and contributions, and my capabilities are underutilized."

Please note that salary (and education) claims invariably get checked, and untruths in either of these areas are grounds for termination with cause, something that will make subsequent job searches that much more difficult. You should know that the interviewer could ask to see a payroll stub or W2 form at the time you start work, or could make the offer dependent on verification of salary. A new employer may request verbal or written confirmation from previous employers or might use an outside verification agency.

In any instance where an employer checks references, credit, or other matters of verification, she is obliged by law to get your written permission. The impossibly small print on the bottom of the job application form— followed by a request for your signature—usually authorizes the employer to do just that.

How much money do you want?

Ask for too much and you might not get an offer; ask for too little and you could be kicking yourself for years. The answer is to *come up with a salary range that puts you in the running, but doesn't nail you down to one specific dollar figure* that you might regret.

All jobs have salary ranges attached to them. Your approach is to come up with a salary range for yourself. Do this by coming up with three different figures:

1. First, given your skills, experience, and location (it costs more to live in Manhattan than it does in Charleston), determine the least you would accept for a suitable job with a stable company.

The least means enough to keep a roof over your head and food on the table.

2. Second, given the same considerations, what would constitute a fair offer for a decent job with a good company—it helps to evaluate what your skills are worth in the current market. There are wide variations based on innumerable factors, but here are some ways you can get a basic idea:
   - Salary calculators such as *www.salary.com* or *www.bls.gov*. Google "salary calculator" and "salary report" and include terms such as your job title, profession, or industry in separate searches.
   - Job postings
   - Headhunters you approach may be able to tell you the salary range for your position within your target location

3. Third, given the same considerations of skills, experience, and location, come up with the figure that would make you smile, drop dead, and go to heaven on the spot.

At the end of this process, you've got three figures: a minimum, a midpoint, and a dream salary. Having come up with these three dollar amounts, kick out the lowest because you can always negotiate downward. This leaves you with a salary range—your midpoint to your high point—that you can give with confidence, "I am looking for somewhere between . . ." Now, like any employer, you have a considered salary range.

Entering Negotiations

Negotiations start when the interviewer brings up the subject of money. Until the interviewer is ready to raise the topic, you should focus on bringing him to that point. Remember that your focus is to get an offer: Nothing is negotiable until everyone is convinced you are the right person for the job. The subject may be introduced with phrases like "How do you think you would like working here?" or "Well, what do you think?"

Career Strategy

Everyone who writes about contract negotiation talks about the money. *Money is important, but your career trajectory more so.*

When you are climbing the professional ladder, sometimes you have to make strategic career moves that have little salary benefit but support long-term planning.

The most important strategic career move I ever made—and it was one that irrevocably changed my life's path—required me to take a 50 percent cut in salary. The guy representing me was Bob Morris, a successful Manhattan headhunter. He gave me the final offer knowing it was a big disappointment. I asked him what he thought I would do; he thought I'd turn it down without a second thought. Instead I accepted it on the spot. I took the hit because, looking at that company at that time, they had no one in my area of expertise who had half my knowledge, plus it got me permanently out of sales, and into training, which gave me wider professional horizons, and at twenty-nine, I was smart enough to know that sales was a young man's game. Most importantly, it fitted into my long-term goals. I did well in the job and it was in that company that I discovered *multitasking*, which in turn led to my first book, and three decades later to you and I talking today.

I tell you this story because *Knock 'em Dead* books are about changing the trajectory of your life, and because it makes two points:

1. New jobs are pivotal points in your life that affect not just this job and the next couple of years, but your whole life going forward. They shouldn't represent decisions made without thought or purely on the basis of salary.
2. If you have a long-term plan for your life, you will be more focused and make smarter decisions. It's okay if your plans change: Heading somewhere—anywhere—with purpose is better than having no sense of direction and no purpose.

When Negotiations Begin

The conversation will then turn to money. The interviewer will ask, "How much do you want?"

If this begins before you've got enough details about the job to negotiate in good faith, you can ask for more information: "I still have a few questions about my responsibilities, and it will be easier to talk about money when I've cleared them up. Could you explain . . ."

If you are ready to negotiate, I recommend a two-step process: The first strives to get the interviewer to put a dollar figure on the table, because you have a stronger negotiating position when you know the employer's range; in the second step you offer your predetermined range.

STEP ONE

Open with, "If I understand the job correctly . . ." and then restate the responsibilities of the job as you understand them, building into your explanation what you know about the role of the job within the department, any initial or special projects, and any special needs that have come to light in your conversations. Your goal is to demonstrate your thorough grasp of the job. You want the interviewer muttering, "Wow, she really gets it!" Your dialogue sounds something like this: "If I'm qualified for this job, which I am because of A, B, C, and D . . . I feel sure you'll make me a fair offer. What is the salary range for this position?"

You can be given a range, and if any part of that range intersects with *your* range, you reply, "Excellent! We certainly have something to talk about, because I was looking for between $ _____ and $ _____. Obviously, I'd like the latter. How close do you think we can get?" or "That's certainly something we can talk about. I'm looking for between $ _____ and $ _____. How much flexibility is there?"

STEP TWO

The interviewer can decline your request and ask again what you want. You reply with your salary range, which maximizes the chances of finding a match and minimizes the odds of asking for too much or too little. Always give a range, extending from your midpoint to your maximum, because a single specific dollar figure traps you.

Once an Offer Is on the Table

When the interviewer names a figure, which has to happen at some point, confirm that this is, in fact, the offer. Because salaries are fairly standardized, the majority of offers will come within your negotiating range. But even if the offer is fair or even exceptional, you can still negotiate.

Career management experts don't agree on negotiation strategy, but we do agree that the first offer is usually fairly close to the final offer and that you can sour negotiations by repeatedly coming back to the well. The state of the job market can impact negotiations too: When supply exceeds demand, negotiating upward is harder. Nevertheless, with an offer on the table, the hiring manager has made the decision that he can hire you and get back to work. He and everyone else wants to be done with this project; negotiate in good faith and your negotiations will be accepted in the same way.

Depending on where the offer is on your predetermined range, you can suggest that their offer is close to your low end and ask, "Is there any room for flexibility here?" You may get a bump since the first figure put on the table often isn't the best that can be offered; and because the employer thinks you're the best person for the job, you needn't worry about negotiating yourself out of a job at this point. The worst that will happen is that the hiring manager will stick to the original offer.

Whatever the initial offer comes in at, always give it one realistic push for more. Then lower the tension by moving away from money and addressing other aspects of the package.

Questions to Evaluate the Job

If you have a plan for professional growth in your core career, you want to land at an outfit that believes in encouraging professional growth. To find out, ask a few questions.

The Job and Its Potential

- How long has the job been open?
- Why is it open? Who held the job last?
- What is she doing now? Promoted, fired, or quit?
- How long was she in that job?
- How many people have held this job in the last three years? Where are they now?
- How often have people been promoted from this position—and how many, and where to?

Other questions that might follow include:

- What does it take to succeed in this job?
- Who fails in this job and why?
- What personality traits do you consider critical to success in this job?
- What kind of training does the company provide/encourage/support?
- How long have you held this position?
- Why did you choose to work here?
- Tell me about your management style.
- How often will we meet?
- How frequent are performance and salary reviews? And what are they based on—standard raises for all, or are they weighted toward merit and performance?
- How does the performance appraisal and reward system work? Exactly how are outstanding employees recognized, judged, and rewarded?

- What is the complete financial package for someone at my level?
- To what extent are the functions of the department recognized as important and worthy of review by upper management? (If upper management takes an interest in the doings of your work group, rest assured that you are in a visible position for recognition and reward.)
- Where and how does my department fit into the company pecking order?
- What does the department hope to achieve in the next two to three years? How will that help the company? How will it be recognized by the company?
- What do you see as the strengths of the department? What do you see as weaknesses that you are looking to turn into strengths?
- What role do you hope I will play in these goals?
- What informal and formal benchmarks will you use to measure my effectiveness and contributions?
- Based on my effectiveness, how long would you anticipate me holding this position? When my position and responsibilities change, what are the possible titles and responsibilities I might grow into?
- What is the official corporate policy on internal promotion? How many people in this department have been promoted from their original positions since joining the company?
- How do you determine when a person is ready for promotion?
- What training and professional development programs are available to help me grow professionally?
- Does the company encourage outside professional development training? Does the company sponsor all or part of any costs?
- What are my potential career paths within the company?
- To what jobs have people with my title risen in the company?
- Who in the company was in this position the shortest length of time? Why? Who has remained in this position the longest? Why?

Corporate Culture

All companies have their own way of doing things—that's corporate culture. Not every corporate culture is for you.

- What is the company's mission? What are the company's goals?
- What approach does this company take to its marketplace?
- What is unique about the way this company operates?
- What is the best thing you know about this company? What is the worst thing you know about this company?
- How does the reporting structure work? What are the accepted channels of communication and how do they work?
- What kinds of checks and balances, reports, or other work-measurement tools are used in the department and company?
- What advice would you give me about fitting into the corporate culture—about understanding the way you do things here?
- Will I be encouraged or discouraged from learning about the company beyond my own department?

Company Growth and Direction

For those concerned about employment stability and career growth, a healthy company is mandatory.

- What expansion is planned for this department, division, or facility?
- What is your value proposition to prospective customers?
- When you lose a deal, to whom do you lose it?
- What markets does the company anticipate developing?
- Does the company have plans for mergers or acquisitions?
- Currently, what new endeavors is the company actively pursuing?
- How do market trends affect company growth and progress? What is being done about them?
- What production and employee layoffs and cutbacks have you experienced in the last three years?

- What production and employee layoffs and cutbacks do you anticipate? How are they likely to affect this department, division, or
facility?
- When was the last corporate reorganization? How did it affect this
department? When will the next corporate reorganization occur?
How will it affect this department?
- Is this department a profit center? How does that affect
remuneration?

Negotiating Benefits

Once a base salary is on the table, and you give it one shot at a bump
upward, move away and ask questions that give you more information
with which to evaluate the opportunity. The next step is to address
benefits and other incentives. These can be an important compensation if the initial offer is lower than you wanted. For instance, you can
ask about:

- A signing bonus
- A performance review after a specified number of days (90/120),
followed by a raise
- A title promotion after a specified period
- A year-end bonus
- Stock options
- 401(k) and other investment-matching programs
- Compensation days for unpaid overtime/travel
- Life insurance
- Financial planning and assistance
- Paid sick leave
- Personal days off
- Profit sharing
- Vacation

You can ask these questions over the phone, or request another meeting to review these points. I prefer the latter because you get to meet everyone as the new member of the team and the boss is buoyant because he can at last get back to work. These factors encourage agreement with reasonable requests, as might a *tiny* worry that you might walk and leave them back at square one.

You may get nothing more than the standard package, but you have nothing to lose and everything to gain. Once the package is straightened out, come back to the base salary one last time: "I want the job, Charlie. I'm excited by the opportunity and working for you and joining the company, but is there anything we can do about the starting salary?" The answer to this question is going to determine what the final offer will be; going to a third round will often sour negotiations.

Employment Obligations and Restrictions

You may accept verbally, but what really matters is the written offer. Pay careful attention to what the company will ask of you in signing the agreement. Employment contracts are legal documents written in clumsy English designed to obfuscate and intimidate the neophyte. You can and should take the time to have it explained, and then take it home and see if you agree with that interpretation; if in doubt, take it to any employment lawyer, because what someone *says* it means is worth nothing. You need to be crystal clear in your own mind about your obligations and the rights you may be signing away.

Your employment contract may include:

Assignment of Inventions
If you create anything during the period of your employment, the company may require you to turn it over. This may include work you do on your own time if it relates to your duties at the company. If you have an entrepreneurial dimension to your life, you may want to seek counsel on this issue.

Non-Disclosure Clauses

Companies will likely require that you not discuss company business with any outside source to prevent the competition from learning company secrets. The language is likely to be general and thus unfavorable to you. If you're concerned about this, try to get the language more specific.

Non-Compete Clauses

The company may want to restrict you from working for competitors, perhaps for an extended period of time after you leave the company. Obviously this can have a negative impact on your future career, since it restricts your employability. Try to make the language more specific—this will create fewer problems for you. Either seek counsel on this or visit employment and labor-law websites for advice on these issues.

Severance

Ask for a severance agreement. A month of salary for every year of employment or every $10,000 of salary is fairly standard. If you sign a non-compete agreement, require that your severance extend through the entire period of the non-compete.

Relocation

Relocation packages vary tremendously, and in recent years many companies have been cutting back on them. You want full moving services if at all possible, but even if you end up with a U-Haul truck, in addition to covering the cost of said truck and a few hundred dollars for incidentals, you can ask for:

- Reimbursement for house-hunting trips before you start. Point out that this will help you hit the ground running as soon as you arrive at the company.
- Temporary housing while you find a permanent place to stay.
- Shipping of autos, boats, etc.

- Cost of a professional moving company to pack and move your possessions.
- Costs related to the selling of a house in one town and buying one in another town.
- Job search assistance for a working spouse.
- Help in finding a new school for the kids.

Accepting the Offer

The process of negotiating the offer may take some time, but when it's concluded, be sure to mention how excited you are about the new job. Reply to the offer in a formal written letter. Begin composing your letter of resignation to your current employer as you prepare to step into a new phase of your career. Never resign your current position until you have an offer in writing.

If you are currently employed, while the new employer wants you onboard as soon as possible, this doesn't mean you should shortchange your current company by failing to give adequate notice. The new employer will understand and respect that you want to leave your current job in a clean and professional way.

Starting the New Job

This book is all about *turning job interviews into job offers*, but in the process, you have gained considerable insights into how to make a success of the new job. But don't take that new job as a cue to let your guard down and forget about career management until the next time you're out of work. If you want to have a truly fulfilling professional and personal life, you need to stay active in career management. That means, among other things, getting off on the right foot at that new job, preparing for the next step up the ladder with professional development programs, and building and maintaining a professional network to help you with your next career move. I talk about these issues of career strategy in detail in *Knock 'em Dead: Secrets & Strategies for Success in an Uncertain World.*

In the meantime, congratulations!! Improving your ability to turn job interviews into job offers will be repaid time and again over the years with more and better offers over the balance of your career. Now go get 'em!

APPENDIX

Age Discrimination in a Youth-Oriented Culture

Concerned about age discrimination? No matter how young you feel inside, it is self-defeating to believe that no one is going to notice that you look nearer to sixty than to thirty. It seems like only yesterday that Abbie Hoffman said, "Never trust anyone over thirty"—and I laughed. Now I am the establishment, and if you are reading this you are probably part of the same club. This appendix is intended for that person who still has the need to compete and who intends to fight a vigorous rearguard action, minimizing the negative impact of age discrimination. In talking about ways to minimize the impact of age discrimination on your job search, I may offend the personal convictions of some about growing old gracefully. I intend no offense; I am simply offering actions you may or may not wish to consider in your personal discrimination battles.

So let's face some of the not-so-pleasant facts.

- You live in a youth-oriented culture, and none of us look as young as we used to.
- The higher you climb professionally, the fewer the opportunities and the tougher the competition.
- You engage in a constant struggle to do your jobs, have lives, and continue your professional education to avoid obsolescence.

- With age and experience you continually cost more.
- You can be seen as know-it-alls and as potential management problems, especially to younger managers.
- You can be seen as lethargic and without drive.

What can you do about age discrimination? Ever since Title VII of the Civil Rights Act of 1964, it has been illegal to discriminate in employment against someone because of his or her age. Nevertheless, it happens. Let's address some things you can impact, short of launching a time-consuming and difficult-to-win lawsuit.

Sometimes interviewers seem to have an irrational (some would say immature) bias against maturity. Sometimes you cause problems for yourselves with your manner, your appearance, and with the way you handle questions. You hear about age discrimination and you see it with your own eyes. When you feel intimidated and become defensive, this only draws attention to the issue. Defensive mannerisms in a job interview can be misinterpreted to mean you're someone with an attitude problem who could present an unwanted management challenge.

With age—if you are lucky—comes maturity, but with it can also come a blind spot to the insecurities you once felt in youth. That younger interviewer may very well be intimidated and defensive, too. Now you have two people feeling uptight and neurotic! Use your maturity to be sensitive to this issue, both in dealing with your own feelings and being alert to the possible discomfort on the interviewer's side of the desk.

The Interviewer's Questions

Interviewers do have some legitimate concerns: Are you a management problem, and are you current with the changes that technology continually delivers to the workplace? It's a fine line you tread: Yes, you want to demonstrate your knowledge and experience as a front-rank senior professional; and no, you can't afford to come across as a know-it-all and thereby a potentially disruptive force.

In such a fast-changing business climate, coming across as a know-it-all has another potential problem: The interviewer may see you as rooted in the past rather than the present. Being current requires more than formal, ongoing professional education classes, it means that you are connected to your profession and its constantly changing ways.

The best way to achieve and maintain this professional currency (pun intended) is to have a presence on LinkedIn and perhaps other professionally oriented social networking sites and to be an active member of one or more professional associations. If you are not currently a member of a professional association, type " _____ associations" into an Internet search engine, replacing the blank with your profession; or, visit the Internet resources page at *www.knockemdead.com*. Take out membership in at least one association and get involved with the local meetings; this will keep you professionally vibrant and provide the opportunity to know and be known by the best connected and most committed professionals in your area—this is the key to the local inner circle of your profession/industry.

Being perceived as a know-it-all raises the specter of a management problem, and manageability is an issue for every job candidate regardless of age (never more so than with executives). You may well be asked questions about management and manageability, how you handle input and criticism, and how you give the same. Consider your approaches to these questions in advance (see the entire interview section), and rehearse how you will handle them.

Another way you can avoid giving the impression of arrogance is with your attitude and the way you answer questions. Here it helps to monitor your body language when you're talking (see the body language chapter) and maintain eye contact to show you are an active listener. Smile—not continually like some gibbering bliss ninny, but enough to give yourself an amiable posture. You should also mirror the interviewer's smiles, pleasantries, and witticisms. They are efforts at friendliness, and you should respond in kind.

Illegal Questions about Age

As it is illegal to discriminate against a job candidate because of age, many questions about age in an interview can be considered illegal.

However, that doesn't stop them being asked, so the question is how to handle them.

You could say, "That's an illegal question, and I'm not going to answer it." Of course, a response like this isn't going to get you a job offer; you sound like a troublemaker already. As I discuss throughout this book, the best way to answer any question is to demonstrate that you understand what is behind it, and at the same time, make a positive statement about yourself in the response.

So what is behind these questions? Actually, they usually mean that the interview is going well—the interviewer is looking at you favorably, probably thinks you can do the job, and is just showing an interest in you as a human being.

Let's step back from a job interview, just for a moment, and imagine yourself at a barbecue. You meet a stranger and make small talk, "Where are you from? What do you do? You married? Kids? You have grandchildren? How old are you?" Questions you have all asked at one time or another, yet if asked during a job interview every one of them could be interpreted as illegal. All too often, these questions at an interview are just the result of someone showing interest in you as a person, like at the barbecue.

So here's one way you could answer the age question: "I'm forty-nine." That's okay as far as it goes, but it doesn't do anything to advance your candidacy, so let's drive straight on to the next and best option, where you answer the question and show that your age adds a plus to your candidacy.

"It's interesting you should ask. I just turned forty-nine. That gives me _____ years in the profession, and _____ years doing exactly the job you're trying to fill. In those years I've gained experience in all kind of situations and environments, made my share of mistakes and learned from them, all on someone else's payroll (smile). I guess the great benefit to my experience and energy level is _____."
Finish with a benefit statement about what you bring to the job.

Even if the age question remains unspoken, it is almost certainly still being asked. In my coaching practice, I tell clients they may consider answering the unspoken question themselves at that point when the interviewer asks, "Do you have any questions?"—if not before. I suggest they personalize an answer along the lines of:

"Jack, if I sat in your chair looking at me, a seasoned professional, I'd have a bunch of age related questions that I couldn't ask. I'd be considering issues like energy, drive, manageabillty, how well you'd get on with a team where everyone looks to be X years younger and I'd be thinking about you keeping current professionally..." You can then proceed, as in the example in the prior paragraph, with the benefits of your experience and maturity as they relate to the job under consideration. You can add comments about these issues too, as they relate to your circumstances.

- My experience means that I have already lived through panics, emergencies, and times when the poop hits the paddle wheel. When crises occur as they do in your business, I've been there and lived through them and learned from the experiences.
- You'll find me a steadying influence who won't get flustered and who will display a calm confidence in your ability to solve the problems as you pull together.
- The average professional stays in a job four years and the younger your workforce the faster the turnover. Turnover is disruptive to meeting the deliverables of your job and this department.
- Hire another Young Turk and you know that: s/he will constantly be haggling for promotions and possibly your job. And that on top of all that, he'll be gone in four years.
- I don't want your job, I want this job and I'm not looking to change again in four years: I just want to find a first-class team, settle down and, over time, earn my place as a trusted member of your inner circle.
- There are benefits to this: I'm competent, conscientious, calm, motivated, and experienced. You'll come to see me as someone who is a positive influence, someone you can rely on to do the work, someone who can be trusted, and most of all someone who will have your back.

You can indeed bring all these benefits to a hiring manager and a department. Take the time to think about each of these points and personalize them to your profession and work experience. The result should be an increased awareness of some special pluses that only someone like you could offer, which should increase your self-confidence.

Make statements like these and you will do more than answer that hiring manager's unspoken questions, you will make a series of unique arguments in favor of your candidacy. You will show yourself to be unusually perceptive, balanced, focused on the issues and to the point, and you'll doubtless make some other pluses besides.

I said earlier that you can raise these issues towards the end of the interview when asked, "Do you have any questions?" However, if you *genuinely* sense that the interviewer is negatively influenced by age issues you can bring up this argument earlier before the interviewer has proved his/her misconceptions to an unarguable certainty. If you see such a situation arising, without messaging that you think the interviewer is an ageist son of a donkey, you can start the conversation earlier with the same, "If I sat in your chair looking at me, a seasoned professional, I'd have a bunch of age related questions that I couldn't ask . . ." and then proceed with your points.

Whatever the point in the interview at which you make your arguments about the merits of hiring an experienced professional, you should be prepared to end with a question that will move the conversation forward; perhaps a question that goes to the very heart of your job, for example, an accountant dealing with accounts receivable might say, "This is all interesting food for thought, but what I'm most curious about right now are the biggest problems in accounts receivable right at the moment. What percentage of payables are aging over thirty days? Over forty-five days?"

But it is not just about answering unspoken questions; your appearance is going to generate other questions.

Can You Keep Up?

Look back to when you were thirty and on the fast track (oh, those golden days of yore), remember how ancient those fifty-year-old wrinklies and crumblies looked: sagging sallow skin, eye bags like Vuitton steamer trunks, and hair sprouting everywhere except on their heads? You live in a youth-oriented telegenic world, and the appearance of your clothes, hair, and skin can say an awful lot about your apparent ability to keep the pace.

This age discrimination in a youth-oriented society is something that will not go away, and that means fighting back: You need to do everything you can to stack the odds in your favor and it starts with facing the facts and doing whatever you feel is appropriate to maintain an air of vibrancy about your appearance.

Women tend to be more sensitive to these issues of appearance than men, who by and large are woefully ignorant of maximizing their appearance. Everything in this section applies to men and women alike—where there is a factor unique to women I will try to address it separately in a box like this:

> As a woman, you will read the following and take the good advice you can from it. You will also appreciate that the somewhat blunt tone and some of the issues are not aimed at you, but at your less evolved male counterpart for whom many of these ideas are possibly new.

Your goal is to look sharp—not for a social date, but sharp for the professional world; so if you need to update some aspects of your wardrobe, there is no time like the present. For more on dress, see Chapter 5.

If you are in an extended job search, money might be too tight to mention, in which case you can get pretty much the same clothes at a fraction of the price by shopping at vintage clothing shops and charity-based thrift stores. These outlets offer an amazing and mostly overlooked resource that I only discovered myself recently when I married an incredibly well-dressed woman who swears by them; now I'm a big believer too.

We now come to appearance issues that I have never before seen discussed in the context of career management. I'm not going to talk to you about having clean nails or well-trimmed hair; you didn't get where you are without knowing these things. What I want to discuss is what you can realistically do to slow down (and in some case reverse) the visible signs of aging, and enhance a look of vibrancy in your appearance.

Hair

With age the texture and shine of your hair changes, and often becomes frizzier. Many of us (mostly men) lose our hair, and mistakenly combing over those last three strands like Homer Simpson, is well . . . being like Homer. The best advice for a man is to crop as short as you like. Not only is cropped (or even shaved) hair currently very fashionable, it is also businesslike, and because a subtle association with sports and the military adds an air of action.

If you are still lucky enough to have hair, it is probably going or has gone gray. If you keep your proudly gray hair, it is not a sign that you no longer have to worry about your appearance. In fact, you have to pay special attention to maintaining an air of vibrancy in other ways. Some men and women can carry their gray hair well and with distinction; others hate it as another visible sign of your mortality. If you dye your hair that's okay too, just be careful how you do it. You may have been a carrot-topped redhead in your teens and twenties, but recreating that color will make you look like nothing other than an unnatural doofus. Hair coloring has to look natural and therefore in balance with the skin it surrounds; you don't fool anybody with the hair color of a youth on a mature body.

Your hair faded gradually over the years, going into increasingly muted shades of its former glory. So you must look at tones somewhere between where you are now, and what you used to look like as a callow youth. You cannot do this with an off-the-shelf bottle of hair color—it is a false economy, as any businesswoman will tell you.

The only way to go is with a hairdresser and an experienced colorist; a professional will do a far better job of giving you a natural color job. Ask to see the big cardboard color charts with samples of artificial hair in graduating colors. Look for the color that was you "back in the day" and then go one or two shades lighter. The colorist will tell you that it won't cover the gray as well, but to my mind that is okay: Color with a little gray looks a whole lot more natural. If it seems fine, the next time you go still try a lighter shade; because the less intense the color, the more natural it will look. If it didn't cover the gray enough, go a shade darker. This way you'll quickly find a color that not only looks good but also is complementary to your face and skin tone.

If you choose to color your hair, this will mean including hair color in a monthly maintenance program along with your regular hair appointment. If you are a man, I don't recommend getting this done at the barbershop. You will need a unisex or ladies' full service salon; you'll get a better cut and the colorists will be more accomplished and have a better choice of products. The greater the color range, the better the opportunity for you to get a color that looks natural. So with this in mind I recommend looking for a salon that uses Goldwell, L'Oreal, or Wella coloring products as these three have the greatest ranges and best reputation for quality and natural colors.

It's the damnedest thing that as the hair gradually disappears from your heads, it sprouts up elsewhere, most noticeably in your ears and noses for men, and on your chins and upper lip for women. This only happens with the passage of the years so it is a clear signal of your aging process; and it is not an attractive look. No one is going to keep your nose hairs under control for you; this is something you will have to do yourself.

At the very least, get a nose hair trimmer, to whack some of that undergrowth. However, this is not the best solution as you can end up with a nasty little stubblefield that will give people the impression you are trying to grow a Hitleresque moustache—not a good idea.

The best and only real solution to this particular manifestation of aging, is to buy a pair of tweezers and pluck the little buggers, painful till you get things under control but very necessary (and probably good for your personal relationships too!). A good pair of tweezers helps, as does a magnifying mirror. For the first few weeks, you'll have to do this religiously every day until you thin things out. Once it's under control, you probably need to do it just once a week as an ongoing maintenance effort. The same applies to hair that grows on or in the ears. You need to get these luxuriant growths under control and then keep things that way.

Eyebrows are another cause for concern, especially for men. As the years have passed your eyebrows have begun to take on a look like

Albert Einstein's or Donald Trump's: wild and bushy and long. This gives an unkempt and aging impression to everyone who sees them.

You have two options: trimming or plucking. If you tip well your hairdresser will often keep your eyebrows trimmed, but again they aren't going to look as natural as when they are plucked. You could easily make this another aspect of your facial hair control regimen. Start with the longest and pluck them out, then do the outer edges where they straggle down towards your ears and cheek bones, then work on the bridge of your nose to give a clean separation and erase that unibrow look so fashionable in prehistoric times. Then, of course, you want to pluck out the gray hairs whenever they appear. It might be worthwhile to start the process by having someone at the salon do your eyebrows for you once; it costs between $15 and $35.

Getting rid of all this unwanted facial hair will have a subtle but significant effect on the youthfulness of your appearance. With this undergrowth gone, and your facial hair under control, there is probably a lot you can do to help your skin look younger.

Skin

If you have left your skin alone, it is probably saggy and sallow in comparison to the skin tone you had when younger; I know this from my own firsthand experience. However, there are things you can do about this that will make you look and feel better.

This is going to be new information for most men, so don't get squeamish, this can really help your appearance and self-confidence.

Healthier, Younger-Looking Skin

Your pores can expand with age and you get skin discoloration from sun damage. Also, men don't clean their faces as carefully as women. Without careful cleansing it is easy to leave dirt and also soap scum; the pores get clogged and will get larger and more unsightly due to oxidation (read: blackheads). The result is dirty, oily dead skin just sitting there on the surface, which helps you look your age. A good idea to combat this is to use an exfoliation treatment on a regular basis; this helps make the skin look smoother and rids it of excess keratin (dead cell buildup). Exfoliate with a soft face brush while cleansing or by using an AHA or BHA product to promote cell turnover.

You also tend to rub your face too vigorously when washing and drying; the tugging and pulling contribute to loss of elasticity—in other words, sagging. This is one of those areas in life where men should pick up some of the habits of women:

- Wash your face thoroughly, ideally with a gentle foam or cream cleanser, depending on skin type: Foam is typically for normal/oily skin, while cream is typically for dry skin.
- Always treat your skin gently, pat (don't rub) it dry.
- Apply moisturizer or sunblock. The sun is the number one factor in skin aging, followed by cigarette smoke and environmental pollutants. A broad-spectrum sunblock, with a formula that blocks UVA (which damage skin cells) and UVB (which burn) rays is recommended.

Different skin types have different needs. The skin types are normal, oily, and dry. And then there are combination skins: normal/oily, oily with dry surface, etc. This latter is caused by overtreatment of oily skin, often with too-harsh cleansers or toners with alcohol.

Many people have combination skin: oily in patches, dry in patches, and normal in patches. If you don't treat these areas separately, in helping one area you'll be damaging another. Once you understand your skin's real needs, you can find products that will really help your skin, and in the process improve your appearance.

Eyes

The skin around the eye area is the thinnest on the entire body and frequently lacks adequate moisture. This only increases the prominence of your wrinkles. Taking care of your skin and moisturizing properly around the eyes won't eradicate these particular signs of aging, but over a month you can achieve a quite noticeable improvement. You will need a separate treatment for this area, as regular moisturizer is not enough for the delicate eye area.

Neck and Hands

The neck and hands also wrinkle and are a dead giveaway of aging. Remember to moisturize your neck and hands, just as you do your face. For hands get a hand cream with at least SPF 8, which will help prevent sun damage and the age spots that come from it. Use fade creams to diminish age spots on your hands and face, a cream with a natural extract such as cranberry or pear leaves (Arbutin) or one with Hydroquinone. When using fade creams, it is easy to over-apply, and this can be harsh on the skin causing redness: Follow the directions.

As the skin becomes more sallow with age, many women try to compensate by applying too much blush, overly pink blush and lip tones, or the wrong shade of foundation. The key is to find a color that looks natural. The correct skin tone foundation should match to your jaw line color; blending is key, so lip color should be complementary and from the same color family as the blush color: warm/warm, or cool/cool.

Five Rules for Maintaining Healthy Skin

Once you have cleaned up your skin and gotten the correct moisturizers and protectants, there are other things you can do to maintain healthy younger-looking skin. Here are five rules for maintaining healthful, glowing, younger-looking skin. You won't look thirty again, but I promise that you will look like you still have a full tank of gas.

RULE ONE

Drink plenty of water. Eight glasses a day, and coffee and caffeinated beverages don't count, as they dehydrate your skin. This is important even in winter, when most people don't think they need as much water. Central heating dehydrates skin and the winter climate makes your skin more prone to chapping and redness, all of which is more visible with your less resilient skin.

RULE TWO

Massage your skin. If you can't get a professional facial on a regular basis (a wonderful indulgence that makes you feel great) learn to do self-massage as this promotes blood flow and helps your circulation. A little research in the beauty section of the bookstore will yield countless books on self-massage technique . . . and it could also turn out to be fun for your partner!

RULE THREE

Exercise. That could be at the gym, outdoor exercise, or at home. Take the stairs, not the elevator. Walk when you can, and get involved in maintaining your house beyond just mowing the lawn. Let's face it, most people in their middle years can probably do with a little more exercise.

With increased exercise comes better circulation, which increases blood flow and lends a healthy glow to your skin. If possible, always try to work out the morning of an interview. Your posture will improve as well, and with the added spring in your step, which sends a signal of vibrancy, you are eradicating the impression of a tired someone who has been carrying the weight of the world on his or her shoulders for half a century.

RULE FOUR

If you are healthy within you will look better on the outside. Eating a balanced diet and taking vitamin supplements can also positively impact the appearance of your skin. You might also consider seeing a nutritionist—you'd be surprised at the number of foods your body might be intolerant to—foods that might be difficult to digest, leading to bloating and skin irritations.

RULE FIVE

Create and maintain a balanced skin care routine, using the advice I've already given you.

Discrimination in a youth-oriented society is something that will not go away. You need to do everything you can to stack the odds in your favor. That means facing the facts and doing whatever you feel is appropriate to maintain an air of vibrancy about your appearance. So on this important appearance issue, the key is to educate yourself and act on the information. You can only look and feel better about yourself as a result.

GENERAL INDEX

INDEX OF INTERVIEW QUESTIONS AND ANSWERS